Lydia Hosto Niebuhr

Lydia Hosto Niebuhr

The Buried History of an Evangelical Matriarch

JOHN CLIFFORD HELT

Edited by Conrad L. Kanagy

Foreword by Deborah Krause

☙PICKWICK *Publications* • Eugene, Oregon

LYDIA HOSTO NIEBUHR
The Buried History of an Evangelical Matriarch

Copyright © 2024 John Clifford Helt. All rights reserved. Except for brief quotations in critical publications or reviews, no part of this book may be reproduced in any manner without prior written permission from the publisher. Write: Permissions, Wipf and Stock Publishers, 199 W. 8th Ave., Suite 3, Eugene, OR 97401.

Pickwick Publications
An Imprint of Wipf and Stock Publishers
199 W. 8th Ave., Suite 3
Eugene, OR 97401

www.wipfandstock.com

PAPERBACK ISBN: 979-8-3852-1005-3
HARDCOVER ISBN: 979-8-3852-1006-0
EBOOK ISBN: 979-8-3852-1007-7

Cataloguing-in-Publication data:

Names: Helt, John Clifford, author. | Kanagy, Conrad L., editor. | Krause, Deborah, foreword.

Title: Lydia Hosto Niebuhr : the buried history of an evangelical matriarch / John Clifford Helt ; edited by Conrad L. Kanagy ; foreword by Deborah Krause.

Description: Eugene, OR : Pickwick Publications, 2024 | Includes bibliographical references and index.

Identifiers: ISBN 979-8-3852-1005-3 (paperback) | ISBN 979-8-3852-1006-0 (hardcover) | ISBN 979-8-3852-1007-7 (ebook)

Subjects: LCSH: Niebuhr, Lydia Hosto.

Classification: BR85 .H42 2024 (paperback) | BR85 .H42 (ebook)

VERSION NUMBER 04/26/24

Unless otherwise indicated, Scripture quotations are taken from the Revised Standard Version of the Bible, copyright 1952 by the Division of Christian Education of the National Council of the Churches of Christ in the United States of America. Used by permission. All rights reserved.

To the loving memory of my parents
and spiritual progenitors of the Evangelical Synod,
a great cloud of witnesses.

Contents

Foreword | ix
Editor's Introduction | xiii
Author's Introduction | xv

1 Exploring Constellations | 1
2 The Little Lady Who's the Spirit of the Home | 17
3 Everywhere in the Church Where She Was Needed | 35
4 Life Need Never Be Sad or Lonely | 61
5 Happiness Is in Our Hands | 83

A Bibliographical Essay | 93
Bibliography | 97

Foreword

THE WORK OF WRITING a biography of an early twentieth-century North American woman poses pitfalls for historians. Women of this period, no matter how talented or accomplished, were largely formed to play supporting roles in service of those in their families and communities. As such, historical treatments that spotlight these women can, on the one hand, be paternalistic, performing the moral equivalent of inviting the women's auxiliary to step out of the kitchen for a round of applause at the close of the congregation's annual meeting luncheon. On the other hand, such work can without sufficient evidence seek to demonstrate the causal role of women in the successes and intellectual ideas of their better-known family members and friends. Both approaches make the mistake of not focusing on their subjects as agents and miss the opportunity to understand women's lived lives within their contexts, thereby illuminating their distinctive vocations and contributions to the world.

John Helt's treatment of Lydia Hosto Niebuhr's life does not fall prey to these extremes. This biographical portrait is set deeply within the context of Lydia's roles among her family and their shared lives in the ministry and mission of congregations, institutions, and schools of the Evangelical Synod of North America, the Evangelical and Reformed Church, and the emerging United Church of Christ and its ecumenical partners. Over the course of her life, Lydia would support her father, Rev. E. J. Hosto; her

Foreword

husband, Rev. Gustav Niebuhr; and her children, in particular Rev. Reinhold Niebuhr (at Bethel Church in Detroit and Union Seminary in New York) and her daughter, Hulda Niebuhr (at McCormick Theological Seminary), in Reinhold's profession as pastor and Reinhold's and Hulda's respective professions as theological educators within these different communities.

In this overview of her life, Helt sketches proportionally and illustrates with historical evidence how Lydia Hosto Niebuhr shared remarkable gifts of organization, administration, communication, imagination, and teaching in support of the various professional roles of her family members at different periods of her life. Indeed, the success attributed to them individually can safely be argued (and was at the time) to be in no small part due to Lydia's efforts. In another era, much like her daughter Hulda, Lydia may well have known professional success in her own right. In her time, the measure of her impact is mediated in and through her relationships and is seen in and through the congregations and communities in which she served and lived. Set amidst the remarkable achievements of her family, Helt presents a compelling outline of Lydia's gifts, as they were for many women of her time, at full flower in service to family and the church.

To bring Lydia's vocational portrait into view, Helt draws upon records of churches and schools in Lincoln, Illinois; Detroit; New York; and Chicago, where her leadership and influence are evidenced in newsletters, meeting minutes, and reports. In addition to archival evidence, he also depends on interviews and other primary sources. Powerfully, some of these resources testify to Lydia's culturally progressive vision of the full personhood of children and the church's call to nurture that in religious and social formation. In his attention to Lydia's particular life and work, Helt produces an outline of how Evangelical and Reformed congregations transformed over the course of the twentieth century from a German immigrant movement to a liberal North American Protestant denomination.

As an American-born child of the immigrant movement, Lydia both embodied and lived out this transformation as an agent

Foreword

of her church's piety (as opposed to Pietism) who was existentially ecumenical, fiercely pragmatic, intellectually open, and socially engaged. As a woman of her time, Lydia Niebuhr pursued her vocation over the course of her long life within but never constrained to different households of her family. As Helt outlines her portrait, Lydia engaged the resources and opportunities of each household context from her parents, to her husband, to her children to express her gifts and bear witness to her faith. The overall outline illumines through the context of her life the costs and impact of what her son H. Richard would later name as the essential purpose of the work of the church in all its endeavors, namely the increase in the world of the love of God and neighbor. Yes, he said it, and she certainly lived it.

Deborah Krause
President
Eden Theological Seminary

Editor's Introduction

THIS BIOGRAPHY IS ABOUT an immigrant's daughter who remained in the shadows of her father, husband, sons, and daughter. But it is also about the theological tradition—German Evangelical Pietism—that shaped her and that she helped to shape. That tradition is also hidden-or buried—for its tendency to embarrass modern sensitivities. As such it remains deeply misunderstood. Grounded in the history of the Prussian Union and the Pietism of the free mission houses of Germany, it is evangelical in a way that is unrecognizable and bears little resemblance to the Evangelicalism of the twenty-first century. In its Pietism, it exudes an irenic approach to theological and doctrinal differences, in a way that is altogether misunderstood. It is focused on peacemaking and deeds of loving and just action in the world, rather than on theological precision.

I note in my recent biography of Walter Brueggemann that Brueggemann claimed a direct through line, going back ninety years, to this irenic Evangelical Pietism, saying that he never wandered far from this spiritual stream as mediated by his pastor father August and the Niebuhrs. Thus, Lydia Hosto Niebuhr is Brueggemann's spiritual progenitor as well, preparing a soil out of which the prophetic callings of the Niebuhr children and Brueggemann and others could emerge. The sad history of Evangelical Pietism is that, like the story of Lydia, it has been buried in the religious landscape of twentieth-century American Protestantism. It is time that

Editor's Introduction

the story of Lydia Hosto Niebuhr be emancipated from a church history that has minimized the story of many of its most important giants simply because they were born at a time when their stories were less valued than the men they supported and the sons they birthed and nurtured in the church. Today there is no excuse for such misogyny in the church.

It is also true that Lydia's children, struggling with what it meant to be German Americans during two world wars with their motherland, did their part to bury and forget the tradition of their childhood. The biography of Lydia Hosto Niebuhr corrects and recalls what has been buried and hidden, and in doing so offers an alternative to the polarization of the political and religious fields of the United States.

This book will stand as a prequel to Brueggemann's story, further helping to answer the questions that I raise about why Brueggemann has made such a significant impact on American society and the church for more than six decades. His answer unequivocally points to German Evangelical Pietism as the source of Brueggemann's fruitfulness. But the current book reveals more deeply what it is about Pietism as mediated by Lydia Hosto Niebuhr that made it such rich soil for the gospel to take hold both then and now. The story of Lydia Hosto Niebuhr as a mediator of a forgotten theological tradition shines a light on the current darkness of culture wars. Could Lydia Hosto Niebuhr be a spiritual progenitor in our twenty-first-century polarization?

Author's Introduction

THE NIEBUHRS HAVE BEEN called the "Trapp family of theology"[1] and "the first family of Christian realism" in North American Protestantism.[2] Matriarch Lydia Hosto Niebuhr was the first lady of this first family. Mother Niebuhr or Mütterchen, as her grandchildren knew her, delivered and nurtured four creative and pioneering children who changed the face of twentieth-century theology, religious education, and journalism. Sons Reinhold and H. Richard often head the list of a theological generation of acknowledged giants. Daughter Hulda, Lydia's firstborn, took her mother's passion for religious education in the parish ministry to the seminary classroom and publication. The eldest son Walter, heir to his mother's artistic gifts, turned these to secular journalism, drama, and filmmaking. German Evangelical Synod pastor husband Gustav Niebuhr, pastor father Eduard Hosto, deaconess sister Adele Hosto, and other kin deeply ground this family tree in the soil of the church. Grandchildren in theology, journalism, and publishing round it out. The biography of this evangelical matriarch provides a wider context for historical understanding of the Niebuhr family. Further, it seeks to secure a place for Lydia Hosto Niebuhr within the history of women in ministry.

Lydia outlived her husband by half a century and survived three of her five children. Hers was a dominant influence across

1. Bingham, *Courage to Change*, 52.
2. Weston, "Ironic Protestantism," 1.

Author's Introduction

three generations of family members engaged in theological vocations. Louis Goebel was a friend and pastoral colleague of the family. Retired from the ministry and presidency of the Evangelical and Reformed Church, Goebel wrote a 1959 memoir in which he remembered the Niebuhr family. He identified Lydia as a praiseworthy matriarch whose family had played a key role in the ecumenical development of his denomination, from the German Evangelical Synod of North America to the union with the German Reformed Church in 1934 and to the formation of the United Church of Christ in 1957. Goebel wrote that the Niebuhr family's contribution had been so great that their mother, Dr. Lydia Niebuhr, had been called the "Queen Bee of American Theologians." He further noted her "gracious, hospitable, warm-hearted spirit."[3]

Twenty years later, theologian Paul Lehmann addressed a convocation at Eden Seminary honoring Mother Niebuhr's three theologian children. Lehmann also referred to her as queen bee but sought to modify the metaphor to establish Lydia as a person "in her own right" who exuded gentleness, humane sensibility, humility, and "unreserved caring." Lehmann elaborated on a theme that more aptly defines the character of this woman whose motherhood extended far beyond her home and immediate family:

> She, more than anyone whom I have ever known, exhibited in her own person her Lord's point in setting a child in the midst of them. Lydia Niebuhr's love for children and their love for her remain in my experience a particularly moving confirmation of Jesus' point, that unless you turn and become like children, you will never enter the kingdom of God.[4]

Lydia's love for children and their love for her kept her young in her faith. Her estate extended her love for children beyond her years, providing a bequest for an ecumenical church agency to do relief work among the children of the world. Daughter-in-law Ursula Niebuhr also recalled, "Many remarked that her gifts

---

3. Goebel, *Recollections*, 52.
4. Lehmann, "Faith of Piety," side A.

Author's Introduction

for dealing with children seemed to make her more and more childlike."[5] A profound and devout simplicity shaped a life of practical faith that bridged two centuries, two cultures and languages, several generations, and a variety of Protestant communities.

Lydia was both typical and unique. Born on Christmas Day, 1869, to German immigrant parents, she remained a bilingual daughter of the parsonage. As a subordinate and dependent, she assisted her pastor father, pastor husband, pastor son, and religious educator daughter across eight decades of parish-based ministry. Though she worked hard and traveled widely during her life, she neither held a paid position of her own nor owned or operated an automobile. Hers was "an entirely derived existence," as Ursula put it.[6] Yet, Lydia pushed the boundaries of her traditional domestic sphere. Her household management always spilled over into wider parish activities, and these flowed into a larger world. Hers was the expansive spirit of an energetic and artistic teaching missionary in the home, parish, denomination, seminary, and society. Consequently, her children embraced an ecumenical and global vision for their vocations, each of which in its own way bridged dichotomies of the sacred and secular, spiritual and political, theological and ethical, and theoretical and practical.

Lydia typified the liberal theological character of the German Evangelical Synod of North America into which she was born and remained exclusively immersed for half of her long life. The irenic and pietistic German Evangelical Synod, like its daughter Lydia, emphasized the formation and development of a dynamic Christian life rather than the transmission of a static orthodoxy. Creed was the servant of character and conscience, rather than the reverse. "The heart makes the theologian" was the cherished motto that Evangelical Synod president Adolf Baltzer learned at the feet of his Berlin professor of church history, J. A. W. Neander.[7] The Evangelical Catechism that nurtured Lydia, her father, and children in the faith was an ecumenical blend of Lutheran

---

5. U. Niebuhr, "Letter," 2.
6. U. Niebuhr, "Letter," 2.
7. Baltzer, *Adolf Baltzer*, 19–20.

Author's Introduction

and Reformed theological symbols. Evangelical Synod historian Carl Schneider wrote in 1925 that it "is not the purpose of the catechism to define our creedal beliefs, but to help in the development and nurture of Christian personalities."[8]

By 1917, Lydia Niebuhr was a widow and took on the organizational life of her son Reinhold's Detroit parish. Among other responsibilities, the matron of the manse was the superintendent of a growing Sunday school and supervisor of its teachers. One of the first women to assume this role in the German Evangelical Synod, Mrs. Niebuhr introduced the principles and methods of a modern program of religious education. About his mother's liberal innovations, Reinhold wrote in a synod publication, "There has been a change of emphasis from subject matter to the object of teaching. Not the textbook but the child is our principal concern. We are teaching the Bible because we recognize it as a guide to spiritual life, and spiritual life is what we want to develop."[9]

Ralph Abele worked alongside Mother Niebuhr and her son at Bethel Evangelical Church in Detroit during the 1920s. In a 1959 biographical essay in the denominational monthly, *United Church Herald*, Abele praised his old friend and colleague, "A Woman Named Lydia," as a humble behind-the-scenes helpmate to daughter Hulda who had recently died. The article divided the five decades of Lydia's widowhood into a drama of three geographic scenes: helping her son Reinhold in Detroit between 1915 and 1928, helping Reinhold and Hulda in New York from 1928 to 1945, and thereafter helping Hulda in Chicago until 1959. This biography will adapt and expand Abele's outline to include five periods of vocational assistantship in ministry during which Lydia lived and worked alongside her father, husband, sons, daughter, and sister.[10]

Chapter 1 visits Miss Lydia Hosto, the German Evangelical Synod parsonage daughter who assisted with the parish duties of her immigrant pastor father in Illinois and California. It examines

8. Brueggemann, *Evangelical Catechism Revisited*, 15–16.
9. Chrystal, *Young Reinhold Niebuhr*, 86.
10. Abele, "Woman Named Lydia."

Author's Introduction

the German American immigrant experience and the unique theological character of the German Evangelical Synod of North America as the context for Lydia Hosto's own experience as a child of two cultures. The chapter ends with her marriage to recent German immigrant Gustav Niebuhr.

Chapter 2 introduces Frau Pastor Gustav Niebuhr, the parsonage wife who managed a household and shaped a family while her husband was itinerant. These twenty-six years of domesticity represent the most important, formative period in the development of the second generation's character. The period ended with the death of Gustav in the spring of 1913, anticipating the demise of German ethnic pride within American culture during the coming war years.

Chapter 3 reveals Mother Niebuhr the Lincoln, Illinois, widow and the Detroit parish assistant who anchored a Niebuhr family ministry. Bethel Evangelical Church enjoyed the tremendous energy and creativity of their pastor's mother as she assumed increasing responsibility for the organizational and educational life of a growing parish from which her son was often absent. In Reinhold's published diary from their Detroit years, he admitted that his mother was in reality a parish deaconess.[11] Bethel Church became a part of the Niebuhr family. Mother Niebuhr embraced the parish as an extension of her own household as her own children established new homes and pursued their careers. Bethel members adopted Reinhold's mother as their own mother pastor. This chapter ends as the son and mother move to New York, where Reinhold joined the faculty of Union Theological Seminary in 1928.

Chapter 4 discloses Mütterchen the grandmother, friend, and teacher of disadvantaged adolescent girls in New York, and organizer of seminary neighborhood children in Chicago. In this long period, her grandchildren were born and married, her children's careers reached their peak, and her two eldest children died. After her son Reinhold's marriage in 1931, Mütterchen joined the neighboring New York household and parish-based educational ministry of daughter Hulda. In 1946, the mother-daughter team

---

11. R. Niebuhr, *Leaves from the Notebook*, 1–2.

Author's Introduction

moved to Chicago, where Hulda would teach first at the Presbyterian College of Christian Education and then at McCormick Theological Seminary. There, at age seventy-six, Lydia adopted a new congregation among the children of the McCormick neighborhood and came to be admired as the fairy godmother of Chalmers Place. The chapter ends with Hulda's death and Lydia's departure from Chicago in 1959.

The concluding chapter tells the story of Lydia's last years of life, spent first with her son and executor H. Richard and his wife Florence in Connecticut, and then with a homecoming to Lincoln, Illinois. There she joined Sister Adele Hosto in the deaconess home with which the Niebuhrs and Hostos had been associated since 1902. Evangelical deaconess Sister Adele, eleventh of the twelve Hosto children, had spent twenty-seven years serving one Chicago parish. But elder sister Lydia imitated the itinerancy of their father and her husband. During her ninety-one years, Lydia lived in at least sixteen different homes in thirteen cities and six states. Yet, hers was a de facto deaconess vocation that shared much in common with Sister Adele. The shape of that vocation will be discussed in the conclusion.

When Lydia was eighty-three years old, she was awarded an honorary doctorate. Significantly, the degree-granting institution was a women's college related to the Presbyterian denomination in which she and her daughter Hulda had worked for the last twenty-five years. The citation for the degree not only acknowledged her role as a mother in nurturing a significant family for church and society, but it also noted her significant vocation as a volunteer, which had included the ministries of parish teacher, musician, visitor, confidante, editor, program coordinator, and promoter. The 1953 Lindenwood College Founders Day Convocation was an exceptional event during a lifetime of otherwise quiet invisibility and public anonymity.

When biographers have examined the Niebuhr family legacy, Lydia has remained dutifully hidden in the background, perpetuating the ideology of women's invisibility and second-class citizenship. Some studies have paid considerable attention to the wider

Author's Introduction

family context, but understandably as a function of disclosing aspects of the principal subject's origins and development. William Chrystal on Gustav, June Bingham and Richard Fox on Reinhold, and Elizabeth Caldwell on Hulda demonstrate the need for a focus on Lydia as the principal subject.

The Chrystal biography, for example, *A Father's Mantle: The Legacy of Gustav Niebuhr*, appropriates the biblical metaphor of the prophetic mantle passed down from Elijah to Elisha. Chrystal shows that the greatness of son Reinhold is largely attributable to his father, the subject of his biography. An important but lesser influence is the mother, who according to Chrystal, was daughter Hulda's role model.[12] Richard Fox, much in the debt of Chrystal's research and conceptual framework for his biography of Reinhold, carries forward the patriarchal-prophetic thesis, going so far as to denigrate the mother's role as "smothering skirts."[13] Fox explains that Reinhold inherited the paternal economic burden of his late father along with the intellectual genius and pastoral vocation and that this legacy at least in part explains the young Niebuhr's journalistic, organizational, and oratorical ambitions: he had to support his mother and siblings and bear the burden of his late father. With Reinhold as the heir of patriarchal responsibility and authority in the family, Mother Niebuhr understandably becomes a dependent appendage, a perspective endorsed by Reinhold's widow, Ursula, who neither regarded her mother-in-law as a woman in her own right nor appreciated her unique gifts or religious background. More positively, June Bingham and Elizabeth Caldwell portray Lydia in a strong and influential supportive role that calls for fuller biographical treatment.[14]

This study discloses a picture of the Niebuhr family and their church background that highlights the common liberal inheritance to which all four children of Lydia and Gustav fell heir: warm and irenic piety that focused on the faithful nurture of persons and

---

12. Chrystal, *Father's Mantle*, 35–41.
13. Fox, *Reinhold Niebuhr*, 173.
14. Bingham, *Courage to Change*, 102–3; Caldwell, *Mysterious Mantle*, 10–34.

Author's Introduction

ecumenical witness in the world rather than the cold transmission of texts or doctrines. This biography seeks to broaden understanding of common social and cultural origins in the Niebuhr family during the lifetime of Lydia Hosto Niebuhr.

In one sense, Lydia personified the ideal nineteenth-century minister's daughter, wife, and mother.[15] She cannot be reconstructed as a prefeminist champion of women's rights or a critic of restrictive gender roles in church or society. As a woman of her time, she seemed to enjoy without questioning the series of secondary, dependent functions that did not directly challenge prevailing doctrines of appropriate women's spheres. "Never had a hankering to do anything else but what I've done," she was quoted as saying about her honorary degree in 1953. "To tell the truth, I never had time to think about it."[16] In a letter to a journalist friend, Lydia lamented that a newspaper account of her recognition had failed to mention the legacy of her husband, who by then had been dead for forty years.[17] Yet, she often told Ursula that she had not missed her late husband because her son Reinhold had taken his place.

Lydia's place, in the writing of her own life, was to stand beside and behind family members. But this hidden place, as Carolyn Heilbrun suggests, proves upon investigation to be fictional. "We have long believed," Heilbrun says, that anonymity "is the proper condition of women."[18] Lydia Niebuhr accepted and perpetuated this ideology, assembling life from the language she was given, a construct born of nineteenth-century Pietism and mediated by the men who dominated her church and family life. She lacked a narrative adequate to tell her own story, one that not only conformed to the job description of a parish deaconess but, more importantly, inspired and helped to shape the fledgling deaconess movement within the Evangelical Synod.[19]

---

15. Sweet, *Minister's Wife*, 29–45.
16. Kimbrough, "Associate Pastor Role."
17. Lydia Niebuhr, "Letter to John Finlayson."
18. Heilbrun, *Writing a Woman's Life*, 12.
19. Heilbrun, *Writing a Woman's Life*, 18–31.

Author's Introduction

It is difficult to recover this woman from her own autobiographical reticence. This biography follows the direction of Anne Firer Scott in *Making the Invisible Woman Visible*. The task of writing an invisible woman's history begins with challenging the apparent anonymity of the subject, whether protected by neglect; by traditional biography of "great men, ideas, or events"; or by the subject's own account. The woman's biographer then struggles with evasive, fugitive sources to disprove his subject's own more evident autobiographical fiction and to reconstruct her life story. As D. H. Lawrence put it, we must trust the tale, not the author.[20] Lydia claimed to be storyless as an author. Although sources for her life-story are few, there is a tale that begins to restore her visibility.[21]

A suggestive illustration of this biographer's challenge comes from Lydia Niebuhr's Detroit days of sharing a parsonage with her son Reinhold. The 1924 Mother's Day Sunday evening educational forum at Bethel Evangelical Church received two quite different titles. Pastor Reinhold Niebuhr would discuss, according to one announcement, "The Mother of a Great Man." Another notice about the same Sunday evening forum revised the title to read, "The Biography of a Great Woman." Given the way Mother Niebuhr manipulated the weekly Bethel church bulletin with her editorial hand, it is likely that the first version represents her interpretation of Reinhold's topic, and the second, more direct version represents his correction.[22] It is unlikely that Pastor Niebuhr explicitly addressed the subject of his own mother, of course, regardless of forum titles. It is also unlikely that the Bethel audience failed to make the implicit connection to their beloved pastor and his mother, and either title would have fit their own hagiographic sense of the matter. In any case, these forum titles represent the Scylla and Charybdis between which the writer of this woman's life must plot a course. Both the invisible woman behind the great family and the great woman whose visibility may be established without reference to her family and church are fictions.

20. Cited in Heilbrun, *Writing a Woman's Life*, 12.
21. Scott, *Making the Invisible Woman*, 12.
22. Bethel Church bulletin, May 11, 1924.

Author's Introduction

Lydia Hosto Niebuhr was blessed with a good measure of the "serenity to accept," "courage to change," and "wisdom to distinguish" between them from Reinhold's famous prayer.[23] This parsonage daughter, wife, and mother thoroughly immersed herself in whatever family task lay at hand. She lived by the educational theory that shaped her teaching and that of her children, as she was in Hulda's words, "absorbed into the context of her own particular life."[24] Yet, Niebuhr's grandchildren, colleagues, and friends admired Lydia for her spiritual independence, inner strength, creativity, and boundless energy. Though one friend's assessment that Lydia was a truly liberated woman may be hyperbole, it is nevertheless indisputable that her peculiar "strength was very important."[25] Though never ordained or recognized by her own denomination, she was a powerful organizer of a vast domestic space that embraced pastoral and educational ministry, offered open hospitality and concern for the world, and anticipated wider acceptance of professional women in Protestant church life. Lydia was a woman in her own right, but it is in relation to her family and her church that she is remembered.

Grandson Richard R. Niebuhr, surrounded by the cloud of witnesses that included his father H. Richard, uncle Reinhold, aunt Hulda, and Mütterchen, his "remarkably strong and gifted grandmother," reflected in his foreword for the biography of his grandfather: "Family legacies, while they can be intricately woven and become deeply cherished 'garments', are woven out of many lives and are of a different order from prophetic mantles."[26] The Niebuhr legacy is indeed "woven out of many lives." Closer inspection of a principal and hitherto invisible thread in that weave reveals a major source of strength within the family fabric.

Metaphorical revision must continue. This matriarch left behind no mantle, but she was prolific in creating patchwork quilts,

23. For Reinhold's famous Serenity Prayer, see Bingham, *Courage to Change*, unnumbered front page.
24. Caldwell, *Mysterious Mantle*, 118.
25. Helen Haroutunian, interview with Elizabeth Caldwell, 1987.
26. Richard R. Niebuhr, in Chrystal, *Father's Mantle*, x.

Author's Introduction

handsewn clothing for herself, her children, her grandchildren and their dolls, knit tablecloths, bedclothes, draperies, woven rag rugs, and dramatic hats. One of her quilts includes the names of her first children, Hulda and Walter, along with other children's names associated with their ministry in the 1890s. Perhaps this piece of handwork represents Lydia's therapy for the long ride by rail from California to Missouri following the death of her infant third child. The patches on this quilt were among her first efforts as a young mother to salvage what was left and incorporate it into something new. But it would not be the last such effort. The remarkably strong and gifted Lydia Mathilde Hosto Niebuhr made a long lifetime of quilts to hold her family and her church together.[27]

27. Richard R. Niebuhr, in Chrystal, *Father's Mantle*, ix–x.

1

Exploring Constellations

LYDIA MATHILDE HOSTO WAS born into the middle of a large family on Christmas Day, 1869. The sixth of twelve children, Lydia lived at the center of a swirling household of activity that tried to keep up with an itinerant father. Pastor Eduard Jakob Hosto traveled widely to establish and strengthen German Evangelical congregations among fellow German Americans in southern Illinois and northern California. The Hosto family moved with him from one parsonage to another and helped to staff his struggling churches until they could spin into a self-sustaining orbit of their own. Lydia learned a dynamic teaching style from her father, of whom she was very fond. "He was a good teacher," she remembered years later, "and did much to make up for the family the shortcomings of formal schooling. For instance, he taught me to play the organ." Lydia also learned to direct choirs, teach Sunday School and recruit, train, and supervise more teachers as enrollments grew, call on the sick, organize and run the women's societies, and help to attract the unchurched. She enjoyed the privilege of her father's attention and extended tutorials, learning his native German and with him the language of his new homeland. Lydia remembered his creativity as a teacher who was interested in the practical application of theology and other disciplines: "In the evenings he would teach me astronomy, occasionally rousing me at night to explore constellations previously studied from charts he had painted on the wall of his study."[1]

"E. J." Hosto had been in the United States for fifteen years at the time of his fifth daughter's birth. He was the firstborn child of a pious Prussian farm family. His mother, born Sofia K. Hurlander of Hanover, was twenty-seven years old at the time of his birth, February 14, 1833, in Westerkappeln, Tecklenburg district, Westphalia. His father, Johann E. Hosto, had been a captain in the Prussian army. Four brothers and two sisters would follow Eduard Jakob, who, at age eighteen, left home to enter the Barmen Missionshaus. Barmen and a Swiss counterpart institution, Basel, were missionary training schools. E. J. Hosto intended to learn the Pietism of the new Protestant union movement and carry it abroad.[2]

Lydia's father entered Barmen in 1851. There he became part of a resurgent German Pietism, reawakening the spiritual fervor associated with Philip Jakob Spener and Auguste Hermann Francke from an earlier century. The German Pietists sought to breathe vitality into the wooden orthodoxy and stale church life of many Protestants, both Lutheran and Reformed. Their religion of the heart de-emphasized sectarian differences and the doctrinal fine points on which many of those differences were based. This cooperative spirit and an evangelical zeal to spread the Christian gospel fed a new ecumenical atmosphere among Protestants in the fiercely independent German states.

Schleiermacher, himself an official on the Reformed side, viewed the confessional differences between the Lutherans and the Reformed Christians in Prussia as insignificant as compared to their practical similarities. He saw the central element in the union as fellowship in the Lord's Supper. Schleiermacher demonstrated

---

1. Chrystal, *Father's Mantle*, 28.

2. Chrystal, *Father's Mantle*, 26–44. On Barmen and Basel mission houses, see Schneider, 1–50.

Exploring Constellations

this aspect of unity by concelebrating Holy Communion with a Lutheran counterpart in Berlin in 1820.[3]

These European roots established an ecumenical precedent for what Lydia's son Reinhold would later call "the highest type of Protestantism."[4] The "best" elements of both mainstream Protestant traditions, namely Lutheran piety and Reformed social ethics, would be combined. The ecumenical liberalism of Schleiermacher provided official theological authorization for the political union in Prussia. But the social force of the union and the mission societies that trained and sent students such as E. J. Hosto was the warm, heartfelt Pietism of the people in the united congregations, including their pastors and missionaries.[5]

The course of study at Barmen ordinarily lasted three years, but after two years, E. J. Hosto became ill and returned home to Westerkappeln to recuperate. During the 1853–1854 academic year, he taught in the Prussian public schools. But when his father died and his mother and siblings "left for America," E. J. Hosto also joined that great migration of more than 5.5 million Germans who came to the United States between 1815 and 1914.[6] In the autumn of 1854, Hosto joined family members already settled and farming in Madison County, Illinois. This German-language settlement, near what is now Alhambra, was about forty miles northeast of St. Louis, Missouri. To learn English, E. J. Hosto went to work in a St. Louis warehouse and attended school in the evening. He helped his brother Henry with the farming, and while plowing behind a team of horses memorized biblical texts and mentally prepared sermons for the local congregation of German immigrants.[7]

The Hosto family helped to transplant the Evangelical Church of the Old Prussian Union on North American soil. Barmen and

---

3. Redeker, *Schleiermacher*, 187–99; Schneider, *German Church*, 399, 401, 412.

4. Chrystal, *Father's Mantle*, 116.

5. Chrystal, *Father's Mantle*, 116.

6. Immigration figures from Moltmann, "Pattern of German Immigration."

7. *Lincoln Daily News-Herald*, "Rev. E.J. Hosto Died"; Alfred Suhre, interview with author, Sept. 1991.

Basel missionary pastors had planted the first Evangelical Union congregations in the 1830s. From New Orleans, where many immigrants landed, and up the Mississippi River to St. Louis, Evangelical churches took root. In 1840, Barmen graduate Louis Nollau called the first meeting of missionary frontier pastors. "For some time," Nollau wrote in his letter of invitation, "a number of German Evangelical brethren who are in charge of United Evangelical congregations have felt in their solitude and isolation the need of fellowship and fraternal cooperation."[8] In the log cabin parsonage of the Gravois Settlement Evangelical Gemeinde (congregation), six solitary and isolated pastors met and organized the German Evangelical Kirchenverein (church union) of the West.

This church society or association began as a fraternity of Evangelical pastors, but after a few years, congregations were admitted to membership, and by 1877 it bore all the marks of a denomination, calling itself the German Evangelical Synod of North America. In the 1880s, when second- and third-generation immigrants came of age in the synod's five hundred churches, an English-language hymnal was introduced. By 1921, when even the most isolated German Americans were forced by world events to examine the language question, the Evangelical Synod embraced more than 1000 pastors and congregations and 822 parochial schools. Of their 376,955 confirmed church members in that year, more than half still attended German-language services, and weekly *Friedensbote* subscribers outnumbered readers of the English alternative, *The Evangelical Herald*, almost four to one.[9] During the First World War, in a period of heightened nativist sensitivity, Reinhold Niebuhr urged the elimination of the word "German" from the denomination's name and discontinued using the language in the congregation he was serving, but the synod remained German Evangelical in name and practice until 1927.[10] With the help of Lydia Niebuhr's other theologian son, Helmut Richard, the Evangelical Synod sought out ecumenical merger partners in the

8. Schneider, *German Church*, 106–7.
9. Kamphausen, *Story of Religious Life*, 166.
10. Fox, *Reinhold Niebuhr*, 41–61.

Exploring Constellations

1920s. Subsequent unions formed the Evangelical and Reformed Church (1934) and the United Church of Christ (1957).[11]

The German Evangelical ecumenism in which Lydia Hosto and her family were nurtured was rooted in the European soil of Pietism and a liberal Protestant union, as we have seen. The German American transplants in the Evangelical Synod of North America long regarded the Prussian union as their Mutterkirche (mother church). The history of the denomination looked to both the 1840 Kirchenverein gathering and the 1817 Prussian fiat as founding moments. But authority among the North American Evangelicals was vested in neither church organization nor political jurisdiction. Practical expressions for Christian unity were uppermost in the minds of Evagelical pastors, and these grew out of their heartfelt Pietism and irenic biblical theology. For example, the earliest creedal statements (1840 and 1848) appealed first to "Holy Scriptures of the Old and New Testaments as the Word of God," but also included the "interpretation of the Holy Scriptures as given in the symbolic books of the Lutheran and the Reformed Church." Where the Augsburg Confession, Luther's Smaller Catechism, and the Heidelberg Catechism disagreed, they allowed, "the German Evangelical Church . . . adheres strictly to the passages of the Holy Scriptures bearing on the subject and avails itself of the liberty of conscience prevailing in the Evangelical Church."[12]

When it came time for the North American Evangelicals to publish their own catechism, their irenic unionist theology suggested a blend of Luther and Heidelberg. In the words of Walter Brueggemann, the Evangelical Catechism of 1847 and its subsequent revisions represented "a curious mixture of dogmatic rigor and pietistic simplicity, a combination which has persistently characterized our Evangelical tradition."[13]

Dogmatic rigor demanded serious theological education of candidates for confirmation as well as ordination. Pietistic simplicity stressed the more subjective development of heartfelt and

---

11. Gunnemann, *History of the UCC.*
12. Horstmann and Wernecke, *Through Four Centuries,* 72.
13. Brueggemann, *Evangelical Catechism Revisited,* 6.

personal faith commitment in every Evangelical church member. Unlike much frontier American revivalism, however, this simple piety was neither anti-intellectual nor excessively individualistic. Its relation to American culture was, using the "Christ and culture" categories of Lydia's youngest child, neither oppositional nor accommodationist.[14] Its Christocentrism may be seen as a theological foil for Helmut Richard and his sister, Hulda Niebuhr, whose work emphasized the sovereignty of the first person of the Trinity.[15] There may be no better single illustration of Evangelical Synod Pietism than the words of the catechism's concluding vow: "Lord, Jesus, for thee I live, for thee I suffer, for thee I die! Lord Jesus, thine will I be in life and death! Grant me, O Lord, thine eternal salvation."[16]

Even more important than the Evangelical Catechism to the nurture of Evangelical Synod church members was the commentary on the catechism, an interpretive handbook for pastors as teachers of the confirmation class. This guide was written by Andreas Irion, who was, in the words of Sydney Ahlstrom, "a fervent, mystical product of Wurttemberg pietism with strong philosophical interests, whose early death robbed the church of an original 'Union theologian.'"[17] Irion demonstrated that the "critical faculty can be united with a reverent spirit," a combination that Reinhold Niebuhr later admired in his father.[18] According to the editor of the Evangelical Synod's theological journal, Andreas Irion "taught our ministers to think while at the same time making them aware that believing means living, not holding opinions."[19] Irion taught at the Evangelical Synod seminary until his premature death at age forty-four. Son Daniel Irion became a long-serving and legendary president of Elmhurst College, the Evangelical Synod pre-seminary located near Chicago, Illinois. Evangelical Synod presidents Adolf

14. Reinhold Niebuhr, *Christ and Culture*, 58–122.
15. McFaul, "Brothers Niebuhr."
16. Evangelical Synod of North America, *Evangelical Catechism* (1929), 73.
17. Ahlstrom, *Religious History*, 755.
18. Reinhold Niebuhr, *Does Civilization Need Religion*, dedication.
19. Dunn et al., *Evangelical and Reformed Church*, 223.

Exploring Constellations

Baltzer (serving 1866–1880) and his son, John Baltzer (serving 1914–1929), also exemplified the enlightened, practical Pietism of the Irions. The Baltzers' and Irions' "Union Protestantism" was a philosophically interested and theologically informed mystical fervor that acknowledged the importance of both the heart and the mind.[20]

In 1850, the Kirchenverein founded an indigenous North American seminary since they could no longer expect Germany and the mission societies to provide all the necessary pastors and teachers for their transplanted union congregations. They built the seminary fifty miles west of the growing city of St. Louis, in the wooded hills of the Missouri River valley near Marthasville. It is here that Pietist Andreas Irion taught his irenic and practical theology, deeply committed to peace and harmony in the body of Christ. Here young theologians learned to take for granted a variety of confessional loyalties among fellow German Americans and to seek common ground amid this diversity. Here pastors and teachers prepared themselves for leading churches trying to steer a narrow course between the Scylla of anticlerical rationalists and hostile frontiersmen on the one hand, and the Charybdis of Lutherans and Roman Catholics on the other. Here they learned the irenic triplet "In essentials unity. In non-essentials liberty. In all things charity."[21] After thirty years in the wilderness, the seminary was moved to the city and became known as Eden. Here Gustav Niebuhr and sons Reinhold and Helmut Richard would be prepared for Evangelical Synod ministry. After fifty years in this location, Eden Seminary moved to suburban Webster Groves. Here Helmut Richard would serve on the faculty for eight years, and Reinhold would serve as a board member for thirty-seven years.[22]

The twofold guiding scriptural motto of the German Evangelicals expressed their irenic ecumenism in the words of Jesus "that they may all be one" (John 17:21) and the apostle Paul in Eph 4:3–6: "eager to maintain the unity of the spirit in the bond of

---

20. Dunn et al., *Evangelical and Reformed Church*, 223.
21. Laaser, *Our Beloved Eden*, 16.
22. Brueggemann, *Ethos and Ecumenism*; Schneider, *History*.

peace. There is one body and one Spirit, just as you were called to the one hope that belongs to your call, one Lord, one faith, one baptism, one God and Father of us all, who is above all, and through all and in all." Clasped hands beneath an open Bible and radiant Easter cross on the face of the official seal of the synod further symbolized the Evangelical ethos. Although this highest type of Protestantism was anti-Catholic, it was unusually ecumenical and socially progressive in relation to its Protestant counterparts. Institutional expressions of diaconal concern for the sick, the orphan, the poor, and the outcast anticipated the social gospel agenda of the Progressive era.

While the Evangelical Kirchenverein of the West was based in St. Louis, there were other Evangelical associations as well, most notably those of Buffalo, New York (German United Evangelical Synod of the East), and Chicago (German United Evangelical Synod of the Northwest). The Chicago-based Synod of the Northwest established a seminary in the 1860s, naming it for Philipp Melanchthon. This name was telling and descriptive of the theological middle ground that the Evangelical union sought to steer between Luther, Zwingli, and Calvin. Melanchthon represented a mediating catholicity in the sixteenth-century Reformation, drawing creatively and inclusively from other Reformers. In 1871, Melanchthon Seminary was reorganized as the pre-seminary for both St. Louis and Chicago synods, anticipating the formal union of the three regional bodies to form the more global German Evangelical Synod of North America in 1877. The pre-seminary evolved to become Elmhurst College, which for more than sixty years served as the exclusive preparatory academy for Eden Seminary. Hence the oral tradition among Evangelicals that their training and destiny were bound to the three *e*'s of Elmhurst, Eden, and Eternity.[23]

The Evangelicals who traced their theological roots to Melanchthon by way of the nineteenth-century Prussian union wanted to distinguish themselves from the so-called "Saxon Lutherans" who rebelled against the union and eventually migrated to form the Missouri Synod Lutheran Church. The unionists wished to be both

---

23. Stanger, "1871–1971," 5.

Exploring Constellations

Lutheran and Reformed, accepting both traditions as normative and evangelical. This concern for unity had both ecclesiological and pastoral dimensions, as we can see in the instructions accompanying young Adolf Baltzer on his missionary assignment from Germany: "He should ... be aware at all times to maintain peace and harmony between his parishioners who will be a mixture of Lutherans and Reformed Christians." The name of the German language weekly news founded in 1850 for Evangelicals, *Der Friedensbote* (peace messenger), and the names Friedens and St. John's given to many Evangelical congregations, also reflected this concern.[24]

In 1860, after six years on North American soil, E. J. Hosto received ordination in the German Evangelical Kirchenverein. In that same year, Hosto married fellow immigrant Clara Elisabeth Kamphoeffner, like his own mother from the German district of Hanover. Clara had been born at Melle there in 1839. At age eleven, Clara had emigrated to New Melle, Missouri, with her family. After a decade in this Midwestern new Germany she married E. J. Hosto and settled in with the other German immigrants to serve the Salem Evangelical congregation of Greencastle/Alhambra, Illinois. During this first Hosto pastorate, the first of their twelve children was born. Son William, born on January 18, 1861, was destined for the ministry himself, and he would become the father of five sons who would also enter the ministry of the Evangelical Synod. Following William were five Hosto daughters born between 1862 and 1869: Elizabeth; Maria, born with epilepsy; Amelia and Johanna, both of whom died as children; and Lydia.[25]

In these seven years, the growing Hosto missionary family made two pastoral moves. In 1865, they left Salem at Greencastle/Alhambra and traveled thirty miles south and west to serve St. John Evangelical Church, Ridge Prairie, Illinois. This St. Clair County congregation was planted in 1853 ten miles east of East St. Louis. During a four-year ministry at Ridge Prairie, E. J. Hosto recorded

24. Baltzer, *Adolf Baltzer*, 31.
25. Nollau, "Clara Elisabeth Hosto" (obituary). Birth order information provided by Ruth Weltge Rasche, St. Louis, as she received it from Sr. Adele Hosto.

Lydia Hosto Niebuhr

forty baptisms, thirty-two confirmations, and eight marriages. No deaths were recorded in this period, and since early records from the Salem church were destroyed by fire, we can only surmise that infant daughters Amelia and Johanna had died before the family's move to Ridge Prairie. In 1869, the Hostos moved thirty miles east to Breese, in Clinton County, Illinois. E. J. Hosto was the third pastor to serve St. John Evangelical Church there, founded in 1858.[26] In July 1869, he, Clara, William, Elizabeth, and Maria moved into the Breese parsonage, an eight-year-old, four-room frame structure on the northwest corner of the church property.[27] Five months later, on December 25, with Christmas texts such as Isaiah's prophecy "For unto us a child is born" fresh in mind, Clara gave birth to another daughter, Lydia Mathilde.

Despite the difficulties of uprooting a young family with a toddler, an ailing epileptic daughter, and Clara seven months pregnant, the Hosto's missionary itinerancy continued. In September of 1871, they returned to their former parish at Ridge Prairie. In November, their son Albert was born and, eight days later, baptized. For four more years there, Pastor Hosto baptized a total of fifty-five, confirmed thirty-eight, and buried fourteen. Daughter Olga, son Friederich (who also died in infancy), and son Emil were born into the family between 1872 and 1880. In 1875 E. J. Hosto moved once again to another Evangelical church named for the fourth evangelist. This one, then seven years old, was in Summerfield, St. Clair County, Illinois, midway between Ridge Prairie and Breese. It is not clear that the family relocated since the commuting distance was only about fifteen miles. But, after two brief years of service at Summerfield, the Hostos moved forty miles to the southwest.[28]

---

26. From records of Illinois United Church of Christ congregations: St. John, Fairview Heights (formerly Ridge Prairie); and St. John, Breese.

27. Description of parsonage in St. John's Evangelical Church, *St. John's Evangelical Church*, 8, 11.

28. According to local historian Gloria Bundy, E. J. Hosto also had a hand in founding evangelical congregations at O'Fallon and Fults, Illinois (Bundy, "Letter").

Exploring Constellations

St. John Evangelical Church in Maeystown, Illinois, called E. J. Hosto to be their pastor in 1877, seventeen years after they were organized and he was ordained by the German Evangelical Synod. This was his sixth pastorate, though there is some evidence linking Hosto to the formation of several other small churches in the area while he was serving those we have named. Maeystown, in Monroe County, was forty miles south and west of Summerfield, and thirty miles south of St. Louis. Here Lydia was confirmed in the Evangelical faith by her pastor father.[29] With a class of nineteen youths, Lydia Hosto took her vow in German to live, suffer, and die for her Lord Jesus. In Maeystown she would have learned the first question and answer in the Evangelical Catechism, that her chief concern in life should be the eternal salvation of her soul.[30] Confirmation day was Palm Sunday, April 1, 1883.

In the year following Lydia's confirmation, the Hosto family followed the westward, overland migration of pioneers' legends, moving from southern Illinois to northern California. The Hostos' dream was neither gold nor other material fortune but the organization of Evangelical churches among the German immigrants there. The Hostos became an active part of the home missions (Innere-Mission) movement, formalized in 1870 by the creation of an Evangelical Synod board. Texas and major urban areas with growing German populations were also targeted for home mission work. Among the German pioneers on the Pacific coast, E. J. Hosto is said to have organized eight Evangelical congregations in California (and perhaps Oregon) during two five-year stays, between 1884 and 1889, and 1892 and 1897. In 1894 a Pacific District of the German Evangelical Synod was organized, and four years later a report accounted for ten churches there receiving subsidies.[31]

The Hosto family at the time of their first California expedition included eight children. Three of their eleven children had

---

29. The confirmation record at Maeystown provides the only known source of Lydia's middle name, Mathilde.

30. Evangelical Synod of North America, *Evangelical Catechism*, 3.

31. On the home missions work of the Evangelical Synod, see Dunn et al., *History*, 147–57.

died in infancy during the late 1860s and early 1870s. Their twelfth and final child, Erwin, was born in 1888 in San Francisco. The two eldest Hosto siblings, William and Elizabeth, did not accompany the others to California in the fall of 1884. Lydia approached her fifteenth birthday as the family left St. Louis for San Francisco. She remembered knitting stockings during the long overland journey by rail.[32] Her younger brother Albert also remembered the journey: "The Hosto family traveled to California from Illinois by train and to a young boy, it seemed an endless trip. There were, however, exciting things to see along the way, and the children often thought of Indians about whom they had heard many stories."[33]

Albert Hosto was twelve years old when the Hostos went west. He later told his children that their grandfather claimed a San Francisco storefront for worship services. He and his brothers and sisters had to "clean the place and whitewash the walls to make it inviting and suitable for worship." He remembered a boy's sense of the adventure of living in California while their father was often away from home:

> On the edge of the town, Grandfather found a small house for the family to occupy. Since he traveled to neighboring settlements to explore the possibility of starting other new churches in the area, Grandmother and the children were often left at home alone for several days at a time. One night while Grandfather was away, the children heard noises outside and, though frightened and kept awake, they were assured by Grandmother that God was watching over them. Imagine their surprise and fear when at dawn they could see a group of Indians sitting in a circle around the house. Soon after that, the Indian leader came to the door and knocked until Grandmother answered. She could not understand his speech, so he finally conveyed in sign language that his people were starving and that he had been told that "the man of God" living in this house would give them food. Grandmother then quickly gathered up all the food she

32. Carol Niebuhr Buchanan, interview with author, Mar. 17, 1993.
33. Rasche, "Uncle Albert Hosto," para. 1.

had and gave it to the Indians, who expressed thanks and departed quietly. But then there was not food for the family, and Grandfather did not return home that day. The children were very, very hungry, but Grandmother assured them again that God was still watching over them and that He would not let them starve. She was, of course, right. Grandfather returned the following day, the pantry was replenished with food, and the family gave thanks.[34]

Lydia later summed up this period in the life of their missionary family, "The fact that Father was always in pioneering country caused hardship but also brought us so much adventure and excitement.... The years of childhood and early womanhood have been a blessing all my life."[35] Father Hosto reported on their situation at the time to inform *Friedensbote* readers and solicit their help: "With God's help I arrived in San Francisco, hale and hearty, on October 11, 1884." His romanticized view of California had met with harsher realities, however. "Conditions here are a little different after all than they looked to be from back in Illinois," Hosto admitted; "there is no lack of work, but how quickly the work will pay off we have to leave to the Master of work in whose great name nothing happens in vain."[36]

Helping with this abundance of work were Clara and their children. Maria, according to her mother's obituary, suffered from birth from epilepsy. She may have inspired Lydia and other members of her family to take an interest in the Evangelical Synod's work with epileptics at the Emmaus Home near Marthasville, Missouri. Maria "left this earth while the family lived in California where she was buried."[37] Lydia would have been the eldest healthy child in their company since William and Elizabeth remained in the Midwest. Lydia followed in the footsteps of Elizabeth, despite the distance separating them, playing the organ for worship services and

---

34. Rasche, "Uncle Albert Hosto," para. 4.
35. L. Niebuhr, "Letter to D. B. Robertson," 1–2.
36. Chrystal, *Father's Mantle*, 29.
37. Nollau, "Clara Elisabeth Hosto."

teaching Sunday School. In 1881, Elizabeth married F. A. Weltge, an Evangelical Synod pastor who then took up home missions work in Kansas. Albert collected the adolescent memories we have already enjoyed. Olga and Emil found West Coast mates, married, and remained in California. Adele was three years old when the Hostos first came to San Francisco. Instead of marriage, she would choose the Evangelical deaconess vocation as a nurse and parish worker. Erwin, born in California, would follow his brother William to Elmhurst College, Eden Seminary, and ordination in the Evangelical Synod. Among the other German transplants in the Hostos' California company was an alcoholic relative whom E. J. and Clara hoped, but failed, to reform.[38]

The Hostos went west with the dream of starting new churches and establishing a colony of German Evangelicals about two hundred miles north of San Francisco, near Whitmore, in Shasta County, California. E. J. Hosto named the place Eudora, "good gift." The homesteaders could claim, after all, 160 acres for $22, and after five years, the land was theirs free and clear. In his second *Friedensbote* progress report to the synod, E. J. wrote with optimism of the immigration of Germans to the West, numbering six to seven thousand per week: "With the colony, it will turn out all right if industrious people will come who don't suffer from homesickness right away."[39]

Among the industrious people who came west with the other transplanted immigrants was young Gustav Niebuhr. Niebuhr had graduated from Eden Seminary and received ordination into the Evangelical Synod ministry. After briefly serving in New Orleans, the synod Board of Home Missions assigned Niebuhr to assist E. J. Hosto in California. A young German American himself, Gustav Niebuhr had followed a path similar to that of his mentor. In fact, one source indicates that this German farmer's son, like Hosto, had studied theology in Germany and took ill, dropping out to emigrate in 1881 at age nineteen. But Chrystal follows the more likely story, that the young immigrant had not intended to pursue

38. Alfred Suhre, interview with author, Sept. 1991.
39. Chrystal, *Father's Mantle*, 30.

a church vocation at all, but rather left his German home and authoritarian father for the secular promised land of American freedom. Niebuhr then experienced a dramatic conversion and calling to ministry while staying with Evangelical relatives in northern Illinois. After his seminary education in St. Louis and brief ministry in Louisiana, Gustav Niebuhr then joined the Hostos' home missions work in San Francisco in 1885.[40]

Chrystal describes the significance of this coincidence: "Beyond all doubt, Gustav's marriage to Lydia Hosto was the most important thing that happened to Niebuhr in California."[41] Gustav's assignment was to care for the Evangelical flock that "Papa" Hosto had gathered on San Francisco's Telegraph Hill and named for the fourth evangelist. Meanwhile, Hosto concentrated his ministerial efforts on the Eudora colony, and despite the two hundred miles between these home missions stations, young Niebuhr and his mentor's daughter fell in love. Lydia Hosto and Gustav Niebuhr married with her father's blessing at Whitmore, California, on May 8, 1887. She was seventeen; he was twenty-four.

Both Lydia's confirmation in the Evangelical faith and Gustav Niebuhr's call to the Evangelical ministry came in the year 1883, a year that also marked the bicentennial of German immigration to North America. This national anniversary was widely celebrated with speeches, publications, official pronouncements, and the dedication of statuary and public monuments, both within and outside German American communities. Oktoberfests and other local German ethnic celebrations had their origins in this bicentennial year. Between 1880 and 1883 nearly one million Germans arrived in the United States. The German was the number-one immigrant group in a growing nation of immigrants.[42] An 1883

---

40. Chrystal, *Father's Mantle*, 11–21. Alternate reading of Gustav Niebuhr's German origins in Stringer, *History of Logan County*, 2:140: "At an early age [Gustav Niebuhr] began studying for the ministry, but on account of ill health was obliged to lay aside his books and in 1881 came to the United States." There is no mention of Niebuhr's conversion and call to the ministry in this version; this account appears to be confused with the biography of E. J. Hosto.

41. Chrystal, *Father's Mantle*, 35–36.

42. Moltmann, "Pattern of German Emmigration."

cartoon parody of this fact showed Uncle Sam, Lady Liberty, and stereotypical representatives of twelve immigrant groups around a lavish table enjoying a Last Supper banquet with a German American as the Christ figure in the center.[43] The 1883 bicentennial marked the peak of German immigration and the self-esteem of many hyphenated Americans.

With Germany's own political fortunes rising after 1870, German Americans cultivated a new pride in their native culture and language. Proposals for communities to adopt English and other Americanizing measures were met with stubborn resistance and arguments about the indigenous spiritual genius of the German "race." But the nationalist nineties would outshout such arguments, sacrificing ethnic pride on the altar of total Americanism. A nativist cultural movement would culminate in the anti-German hostility of Theodore Roosevelt, who advised shooting or hanging any German American found guilty of the moral treason of divided loyalty, not fully accepting the motto of "America for Americans."[44]

The new lives of native-born German American Lydia Hosto and her German immigrant husband Gustav Niebuhr would grow in a social medium increasingly hostile to their kind. Outside the constellation of their own German Evangelical Synod community, the Hosto-Niebuhr clan would be regarded as strangers in their own land. But within it, they were not always comfortable either. In the classic paradigm later developed by the youngest of the Niebuhr children, the family and their church would live on the string of a pendulum swinging between Christ and culture.[45] Finding a meaningful place and making a difference within a wider church and cultural circle would become the identifying marks of the children born into the union of Lydia Hosto and Gustav Niebuhr.

43. Conzen, "German-Americans," 132.

44. Higham, *Strangers in the Land*, 94–163; Hansen, *Immigrant in American History*, 145; Schmidt, "Rhetoric of Survival."

45. Reinhold Niebuhr, *Christ and Culture*, ix.

2

The Little Lady Who's the Spirit of the Home

LYDIA HOSTO'S MOTHER, CLARA, was pregnant with her last child in 1887 when Lydia married Gustav Niebuhr. Lydia's much-admired elder siblings, William and Elizabeth, could not attend her California wedding. Sister Elizabeth had married an Evangelical Synod pastor in 1881 and accompanied him to Kansas, playing the organ for his churches and, like her mother, rearing twelve children. Brother William was serving an Evangelical Synod parish in Smithton, Illinois, where he married only months after his sister Lydia. Though separated by miles and mountains, William and Elizabeth must have reinforced the attraction of their parents' experience as a model for Lydia's own marital choice. She would follow her mother and sister, especially, into the role of Evangelical Synod Frau Pastor. The great organizational skill and creative energy in motherhood, domestic management, and parish ministry, for which Lydia herself would become known and admired, came naturally.[1]

---

1. Jerger, "Pastor Friederich"; W. "Mrs. Elizabeth Anna [Hosto] Weltge"; *Belleville News-Democrat*, "Rev. W. H. Hosto."

Lydia Hosto Niebuhr

Despite distances separating family members, the Hostos and Niebuhrs maintained close ties. Across two generations, matriarchs established and defined the itinerant and dispersed family center, even from afar. In California during the late 1880s, it was Clara Hosto's role. In 1922, when Lydia Hosto Niebuhr lived and worked with her son Reinhold in Detroit, her daughter Hulda lived in Boston. For Mother Niebuhr's fifty-third birthday, Hulda composed a poem that celebrated Lydia as "The Spirit of the Home." Following two stanzas of lament that Boston's culture, impressive buildings, ships, and automobiles "don't spell home to me," Hulda concluded:

> But there is a little lady
> Living where I must not be
> Living in the place I come from
> And her name spells home to me.
>
> She can love you though she knows you,
> Though she sees much froth and foam,
> Hold you to the best that's in you—
> She's the spirit of the home.
>
> I'm glad that lady's spirit
> Is not tied to any place
> It can help to make at-home-ness
> Though I cannot see her face.
>
> I don't need the ships and autos
> Mammoth buildings, spire, and dome,
> Let me have the little lady
> Who's the spirit of the home.[2]

The "little lady" was small in stature, reaching no more than five feet, two inches in height.[3] But her spiritual reach was extensive. After her marriage, Gustav Niebuhr's struggling mission church began to flourish. Chrystal says, "Lydia Niebuhr was deeply spiritual, and she quickly became an indispensable part of Gustav's ministry . . . a striking woman who stood out in many

---

2. Hulda Niebuhr, in Caldwell, *Mysterious Mantle*, 33.
3. Carol Niebuhr Buchanan, interview with author, Mar. 17, 1993.

The Little Lady Who's the Spirit of the Home

ways."[4] Richard Fox claims even more for her: "Before the marriage, Gustav had sometimes preached to congregations of two or three. With Lydia's full-time aid—and musical talent—his parish began to grow. Lydia knew all about church operations . . . [and] ran her parish tasks with discipline and enthusiasm. Like her husband, she reveled in work."[5] As for her father, mother, brother, and sister, for Lydia Hosto Niebuhr, Evangelical Synod ministry mingled naturally and inextricably with family life.

In San Francisco, on March 9, 1889, Lydia gave birth to their first child, a daughter. Lydia and Gustav honored their mothers by naming their firstborn after Clara Kamphoeffner Hosto and Augusta Stelter Niebuhr. But Clara Augusta Hulda Niebuhr would be known simply as Hulda. Eduard Friedrich Walter came thirteen months later. Following the established pattern, his names honored his grandfathers, Eduard Hosto and Friedrich Niebuhr, and he would be known as Walter. Another son, Herbert Barthold Gregory, died at six weeks of age in 1891 as the family was preparing to leave California.[6]

Hulda's earliest memory was that of her grieving mother crying at the loss of this infant child and her father trying desperately to comfort her.[7] But Lydia was pregnant again when the young family boarded the train for Missouri. The Evangelical Synod Board for Home Missions had work for the Niebuhrs back in the Midwest. Gustav was assigned to be pastor of Immanuel Evangelical Church in Wright City, Missouri, fifty miles west of St. Louis. Like his father-in-law and mentor E. J. Hosto, Gustav Niebuhr was to become an energetic and effective itinerant minister and wandering missionary, establishing new congregations, reviving others, and developing interest in and support for the mission of the German Evangelical Synod.

Perhaps the most remarkable local events of the Niebuhrs' four years in Wright City were the births of Karl Paul Reinhold in

---

4. Chrystal, *Father's Mantle*, 36.
5. Fox, *Reinhold Niebuhr*, 5.
6. R. Gustav Niebuhr, "Letter."
7. Bingham, *Courage to Change*, 52.

Lydia Hosto Niebuhr

June, 1892, and Helmut Richard in September 1894. Yet, a century after these events, local memory has relegated their significance to a cross-stitched Immanuel Church wall hanging of Reinhold's Serenity Prayer, a hanging that confuses the family name with the Niebuhrs who once owned the horse-drawn coach works in town.[8] An apocryphal tale is also told of a twentieth-century researcher who came to Wright City to explore the social origins of the famed family of theologians. When an elderly member of the congregation was asked about the Niebuhrs, her answer admitted some recollection of a memorable pastor of that name who had served them before the turn of the century and then went on to do great things. She added, asking the interviewer, "And didn't Rev. Niebuhr have a couple of sons who also went into the ministry?"[9]

In 1895, the Niebuhr family moved forty miles further eastward, to St. Charles on the Missouri River. Gustav became the pastor of St. John Evangelical Church there, but his traveling for the sake of the home mission work of the synod continued. Hulda remembered parsonage life there:

> As young children, we had a large domain in St. Charles—arbors of various kinds in which to set up all sorts of enterprises, the heritage of a Swiss pastor family who raised grapes wherever there was any room. There was an enormous apple tree into which we would crawl with our favorite books. There was a "Gartenhaus," with a built-in table and benches all around where I used to sew doll clothes with my friends but the boys spent more time in the schoolyard adjoining.[10]

After four years with the congregation of St. John, the family moved out of the parsonage to a house a block away in St. Charles. Adelheid Rabine, who would later marry Gustav's successor at St. John Church, Paul Allrich, moved in as Lydia's household and childcare helper, while Gustav became the full-time traveling representative for the Evangelical Synod's Emmaus Home. Years later,

---

8. S. Brown, "Paradoxical Pastor."
9. McGuire, "Few in Wright City."
10. Hulda Niebuhr, "Letter to June Bingham," 2.

the daughter of this Niebuhr housekeeper remembered Gustav as just like his son, Reinhold, never home and always on the move.[11]

The Emmaus Home, then known as an asylum, was a refuge for the "epileptic and feebleminded."[12] Gustav Niebuhr was among the founders of Emmaus, a benevolent institution patterned after the German Bethel bei Bielefeld. The first Emmaus campus was near Marthasville, Missouri, utilizing the vacant buildings of the Evangelical Synod seminary that moved to St. Louis in the 1880s. Niebuhr's task was to raise funds to build an adequate facility for a second campus to be developed on land purchased in St. Charles. While in California, Niebuhr became interested in the German Innere-Mission movement of church-sponsored social welfare agencies. Evangelical Synod home missions must not stop with organizing new congregations, he now believed. The church must reach out to care for those whom society has neglected. Perhaps the sad experience of Lydia's sister, Maria, born with epilepsy and buried in California, moved Gustav to action, founding and funding Emmaus and seeking to broaden the synod's interest in home mission work.[13]

We do know that Gustav Niebuhr, the home missions advocate, saw little of his wife and four children between 1899 and 1902. It fell to Lydia to attend to Hulda, Walter, "Reiny," and "Hem," in 1902 ranging in age from ten to five years old. In Wright City and St. Charles, Lydia provided a stationary counterpart and stable base for an itinerant husband and father. Home missions meant travel to Gustav Niebuhr, much as it had meant to Lydia's father, E. J. Hosto. After the successful fundraising and dedication of the new Emmaus building in 1901, Gustav was sent away from his Missouri home to serve struggling Evangelical Synod churches as far away as Utah and Idaho. Lydia and the children stayed behind in St. Charles.[14] Thirty years later, Reinhold prefaced his published pastoral diary with remarks that may be grounded in a lingering bitterness over

---

11. Adelheid Allrich, interview with author, Sept. 20, 1991.
12. Chrystal, *Father's Mantle*, 46.
13. Chrystal, *Father's Mantle*, 45–62.
14. Chrystal, *Father's Mantle*, 64–76.

his father's long absences from an adoring nine-year-old son. Reinhold characterized pastoral ministry as a balancing act between the statesmanship of the accountable resident and the prophetic critique that an "irresponsible itinerancy supplies." Despite his own imitation of his father's and maternal grandfather's itinerancy as a pastor, Reinhold said, "No amount of pressure from an itinerant 'prophet' can change the fact that a minister is bound to be a statesman as much as a prophet, dealing with situations as well as principles." His mother became the "accountable resident" who dealt effectively with the domestic "situations" that made possible "prophetic critique" and "irresponsible itinerancy."[15]

Reinhold, always one to regard family life romantically, once used a sermon illustration from this period in the young Niebuhr family's life. This reconstructed homiletical memory, translated from German, suggests that the young Reinhold's parents, despite his father's long absences, nevertheless worked effectively together as partners.

> As a child I once spent a day with my grandmother. Toward evening, a severe storm began. "Now how will you get home, child?" the old woman asked. But then my father came to fetch me. He had a big blue coat, as men wore at that time, and as we left he said, "Come under here." I slipped under the coat, grabbed his hand, and off we went. I couldn't see anything as we splashed through puddles and mire. I heard the rain and the thunderclaps and I seized my father's hand more tightly. But I would have been a fool if I had complained that it was so dark around me. After all, it was my father's coat, protecting me from the weather that made it dark. Father saw the path; I knew that . . . and when the coat parted, we were at home! I looked into my mother's cheerful face and at our bright, warm room, and everything was as pleasant and cozy as only home can be! Of course, Father had brought me home. Where else should he have brought me? So it is with our Heavenly Father. If only we trust

---

15. Reinhold Niebuhr, *Leaves from the Notebook*, xiii.

The Little Lady Who's the Spirit of the Home

him, he takes us under his wings and leads us through storm and tempest.[16]

A less idealized story from this period illustrates a more tragic feature of family life at the turn of the century. Elizabeth Hosto Weltge had named one of her twelve children after her younger sister, Lydia Hosto Niebuhr. During a scarlet fever epidemic in 1901, eleven-year-old Lydia Weltge died. Grandmother Clara Hosto, who lost four of her own twelve children to infant and childhood disease, wrote in her letter of condolence to her grieving daughter Elizabeth, "I know this from personal experience, how it hurts when you bury one of your loved ones in the grave. It is as if a piece of your heart was torn." The sympathy then turned to pious counsel: "But when we think how good it is for dear Lydia, to trade heaven for this poor earth; I beg you dear heart not to worry, as the dear child received no harm, but a nice heritage. Let that be your hope, dear Elizabeth; that you have a little angel in heaven."[17] Clara Hosto, crippled with arthritis as well as a grandmother's broken heart, wrote these words (in German) in May. Four months later, in September of 1901, she died. She was sixty-two years old.

Clara Kamphoeffner Hosto was buried in the cemetery adjacent to the remote Zoar Evangelical Church, New Hanover, Illinois, where she and her husband had been serving since returning from their second California missionary expedition (1892–97). Lydia must have wondered if her own fate, like her mother's, would be to raise a large family without much help from her traveling husband, move frequently from place to place, suffer crippling illness and more familial heartache, and die at a relatively young age. During the winter of 1901–2, Lydia's mother was dead and her husband was in Utah. But in the spring she learned that Gustav was being considered for a professorship at Eden Seminary in St. Louis, promising a more settled family life. Upon his return to the Midwest, however, Gustav learned that the position had been given to a German university–trained candidate instead. Later in

---

16. Chrystal, "Father Saw the Path," n.p.
17. C. Hosto, "Letter to Elizabeth Weltge."

1902, the call to a more settled family life for the Niebuhrs came from Lincoln, Illinois. From St. Charles, they moved across the Missouri and Mississippi Rivers and halfway to Chicago.[18]

In Lincoln, the pastor of St. John Evangelical Church was also to be superintendent of the new Evangelical Deaconess Home and Hospital. The home and hospital began when two St. Louis deaconesses were sent to Lincoln during an 1898 typhoid fever epidemic. A year later the St. John's Evangelical Deaconess Society was formed. In 1900 the society laid the cornerstone for the St. John's Evangelical Deaconess Home and Hospital. Two years later, Gustav Niebuhr's predecessor, F. W. Schnathorst, intoned the dedication for the new brick building: "May in this institution true faith, the right fear of God, and the upright serving of social love always flourish."[19]

J. U. Schneider, an Evansville, Indiana, Evangelical Synod professor, spoke of the "underlying principle" that shaped the wider deaconess movement and breathed life and the spirit of service into its institutions. Schneider also sought recruits.

> This is an appeal to those noble-hearted women who are able to pass beyond what they share with the lower orders of creation, and to soar to those regions where as intelligent, God-knowing servants, they are ever ready to do good to all men in universal good will. . . . She takes the pledge of obedience, willingness, and faithfulness after having been thoroughly prepared for the work. She offers her service to Christ. This is the underlying principle.[20]

Later in 1902, the Niebuhr family moved to Lincoln. Gustav was thirty-nine when he assumed responsibility for the new deaconess home, hospital, and society, along with the pastorate of St. John Church. Lydia was thirty-two when she returned to the state of her birth, her first fifteen years, and where her father and brother continued in the Evangelical Synod ministry. Hulda and Walter approached adolescence. "Reiny" was ten. "Hem" was

18. Chrystal, *Father's Mantle*, 74–76.
19. Gimbel et al., *Story of St. John*, 21.
20. Gimbel et al., *Story of St. John*, 21.

The Little Lady Who's the Spirit of the Home

eight. The Niebuhrs quickly became a leading family among the seven thousand German Americans of Logan County. But their interests and activities extended far beyond the parochial.[21]

Gustav held a prominent and influential position in the Evangelical Synod. For four of his eleven years in Lincoln, he was president of the North Illinois District of the denomination. Lincoln was a convenient midpoint between the two urban centers of Chicago and St. Louis and their concentrations of synod congregations. (An old quip about these centers, as expressed by a Chicagoan, echoed the days before there was a united synod of North America: "If St. Louis is the seat of the Synod, then Chicago is its head.") Lydia began to exercise a wider reach into the Evangelical Synod family. She was a magnetic hostess in the St. John parsonage, which often entertained synod and deaconess society leaders. The name Lydia Niebuhr became synonymous with hospitality.[22]

The Niebuhrs moved to Lincoln on the congregation's promise to build a new parsonage for the pastor's large and unpredictable household. While under construction, the family lived in the new deaconess building, where bonds between the sisters and the Niebuhrs were cemented early. Completed in 1903, the nine-room, two-story frame house on a shady lot next door to the church provided ample space for the family and their many invited and uninvited guests. Hulda later recalled an endless number of guests, some of whom were hoboes who, like the Native American visitors to the Hostos in California twenty years earlier, were not turned away empty handed. Reinhold's first biographer, June Bingham, praised Lydia for her capacity to manage this open-ended domestic space, saying the Lincoln pastor's wife and mother of four had so much energy, laughter, and expertise "in cooking, sewing, and toy-making, that her large and unpredictable household did not overpower her."[23]

Lydia's roles as mother and pastoral assistant expanded with the need. Besides playing the organ for Sunday worship

21. Fox, *Reinhold Niebuhr*, 1–21.
22. Goebel, *Recollections*, 52.
23. Bingham, *Courage to Change*, 53.

and working with the Sunday school, she served as secretary of the Frauenverein (women's group) and as chief leader and chaperone for the Jungenverein (youth group). Lydia was one of four laywomen on the thirteen-member Deaconess Hospital board of trustees. She was the first woman superintendent of the Home Visitation Department, an auxiliary of the Sunday school. She also filled in for family members. For instance, son Walter became the scoutmaster of the St. John's Boy Scout Troop Six, organized in 1912, just two years after the founding of the National Boy Scouts of America. During campouts, Walter worked in his Lincoln newspaper office, and Lydia directed camp activities for the day until the scoutmaster arrived.[24]

Much was expected of the turn-of-the-century housewife and minister's wife in any case, but Lydia Hosto Niebuhr surpassed ordinary expectations. She was constantly helping and organizing, as a hospital board member, Sunday school teacher, superintendent of the home department, and officer of the women's society.

The lines between home and church blurred in the Niebuhr household. Lydia had a knack for creativity and loose parental supervision, which allowed childhood play delicately balanced between freedom and direction. She fastened heavy ropes to the barn rafters for swinging and gave the children old mattresses to bounce on. On the evening of the monthly hospital board meeting, which both mother and father attended, the children were free, according to Hulda, "until all hours to play 'circus' or 'World's Fair' or 'Chautauqua.' . . . I'm sorry for children today who have to play under supervision," Hulda went on to say in reflection, "Our school work was set, with lots of memorizing, but our play was free."[25]

Reinhold described a similar picture of a "mother who had real skill in arranging for childish play so that my early childhood was happy in the love of my mother." Lydia reveled in the management of her household—the family band (each child played an instrument) and daily devotions, the kind discipline, the parties

24. Evangelische St. Johannes Gemeinde, *Souvenir zum Goldenen Jubilaum*, 8–18.

25. Bingham, *Courage to Change*, 59.

The Little Lady Who's the Spirit of the Home

and recreation. She fed and reproduced the family throughout her life. Her household would never be without the laughter of children, and her own maturity simply brought out more of the child in her.[26]

Lydia herself remembered those early parsonage days when the children were young: "They were never made to feel that because they were the preacher's children, they were terribly restricted in their activities. I think that's a big mistake."[27] Lydia believed in expressive activity, as she would later put it in an address to a national Sunday school convention.[28] Each of her children was in some way encouraged to break free from the provincialism of Lincoln's culture and that of the German Evangelical Synod. Hulda recalled that her three brothers and their closest friends played in a brass band that practiced in the basement of the church. The band leader was a "pietistic immigrant miner" who always wanted his group to play religious hymns. When the boys' repeated appeals to play marches and other secular music were denied, they boycotted rehearsals and the ensemble disbanded.[29]

Lydia used English with St. John young people and helped her husband, whose primary language remained German. St. John church member Irene Kurtz was in the last confirmation class to be confirmed by Pastor Gustav Niebuhr. She was one of only two youths in her class who spoke English rather than German at home. The parochial school had a rule that only German should be spoken on the playground. Kurtz recalled an incident on the playground when the parochial school teacher, Margaretha Duect, caught her using English and fined her five pennies. Ms. Kurtz's father thought the action too severe and appealed directly to Pastor Niebuhr to reduce or forgive the fine. Since he was trying at that time to learn English himself, Gustav said, he knew how difficult it was for Irene

---

26. Reinhold Niebuhr, *Reminiscences of Reinhold Niebuhr*, 1.
27. Kimbrough, "Associate Pastor Role," para. 3.
28. L. Niebuhr, "Week-Day Activities," 131.
29. Hulda Niebuhr, "Letter to June Bingham," 1.

to speak only German, especially while enjoying the freedom of play. He overruled the teacher and forgave the child's fine.[30]

In Lincoln, the Niebuhrs became outspoken advocates for the deaconess movement throughout the Evangelical Synod. Like the Emmaus Home, the deaconess movement was a feature of home mission work patterned after effective German models. Kaiserwerth pastor Theodor Fliedner had enlisted women to work with society's victims, living by a threefold vision of Christian servanthood: servants of the Lord Jesus, servants of the sick and poor for Jesus' sake, and servants to each other.[31] The deaconess movement in the Evangelical Synod encouraged single women to receive special training and take vows as nurses to serve in hospitals and other institutions being established throughout the synod. Gustav Niebuhr believed in this "churchly vocation," thinking it provided women with the opportunity to utilize their "special gifts for service."[32] He wanted to formalize, systematize, and authorize the kind of womanhood he admired in his wife. More women like Lydia would help the church in its application of the gospel and protect womanhood from the exploitative ills of society. The deaconess movement offered an acceptable alternative to what Gustav regarded as socially dangerous morally destructive secular career paths opening to American women.[33]

While the Lincoln deaconess society began with hospital nursing as its focus, the Niebuhrs helped to expand the ministry of deaconesses to parish work. The parish deaconess would assist the pastor, "extending and promoting the spiritual welfare of the church among its members." She would give full-time pastoral care, visiting regularly in homes on behalf of the pastor, the Sunday school, and its home department; visit the sick and provide day and night nursing care for the homebound; and offer sewing and cooking instruction in members' homes. Home economist, social worker, dietitian, counselor, adviser, parochial and Sunday school

---

30. Irene Kurtz, interview with author, Sept. 20, 1991.
31. Chrystal, *Father's Mantle*, 79.
32. Chrystal, *Father's Mantle*, 79.
33. Chrystal, *Father's Mantle*, 77–94.

The Little Lady Who's the Spirit of the Home

truant officer, and nurse, the parish deaconess would thoroughly extend the ministry of the church into the homes of its members and neighbors. "This was the service of love and mercy, administering the charities of the church."[34]

Lydia closely but informally appropriated much of this evangelical deaconess model of servant discipleship. Or, perhaps it is more accurate to say that it was her natural gifts and developed expertise as an interested and active child of the Evangelical parsonage that guided her husband's vision of the deaconess vocation. In any case, Lydia and daughter Hulda lived much of their lives as parish deaconesses, though they never took the vows to be officially consecrated in the vocation. But Lydia's youngest sister, Adele Hosto, was so consecrated at St. John, Lincoln, in 1914. Clara and E. J. Hosto had named their last daughter, born in 1881, after their good friend, Adelheid Schmidt, a former deaconess who helped to plant the seed for the movement in Lincoln. At the time of Gustav Niebuhr's alarming death in 1913, Adele Hosto was a deaconess probationer in Lincoln. The *Daily News-Herald* obituary (perhaps written by son Walter) told the story of the pastor, his sister-in-law, and the deaconess work that bound them together: "Reverend Niebuhr was among the first to agitate for the re-establishment of congregational deaconesses for work among the members, and the two sisters who were in constant attendance at his bedside during his last illness, Sister Adele Hosto and Sister Charlotte Pfeiffer, were the first two who were started in this work."[35]

When Sister Adele was installed in 1915 to serve a large Chicago congregation, she was the first parish deaconess consecrated in the North Illinois District and only the second in the whole of the Evangelical Synod. She served Friedens Evangelical Church (later known as Peace Memorial) for twenty-seven years. When she returned to Lincoln in 1942, Sister Adele served as interim hospital administrator, official hospital hostess, housemother for the nurses' residence, and member of the hospital's general nursing staff;

---

34. Gimbel et al., *Story of St. John*, 35.
35. Gimbel et al., *Story of St. John*, 34.

became active in St. John church and Sunday school; and at the end of her sister Lydia's life, attended her deathbed as she had Gustav's.[36]

Lydia ministered in the shadow of her husband during twenty-six years of marriage, just as Sister Adele Hosto followed her "churchly vocation"[37] of servanthood as an authorized deaconess. Here and throughout her long life, Lydia accepted the domestic and dependent roles she was given. Her subordinate lot squared with some of the most restrictive definitions of women's appropriate sphere that were operative in the early twentieth century. When her pastor husband died, she quickly took up with her pastor son, Reinhold, smoothly transferring her energies and skills to another place. With him in his Detroit parish, Lydia worked quietly behind the scenes as a humble, self-effacing servant, "administering the charities of the Church."[38] Reinhold later recalled, "In my parish in Detroit, she was, in effect, a parish deaconess. . . . I started very early to . . . give lectures in the colleges, all of which was made possible by the fact that my mother was, in effect, assistant pastor."[39] Though she was "in effect" both parish deaconess and assistant pastor, she never received a salary. Though she lived more than a dozen years in Henry Ford's Motor City, she never learned to drive an automobile. She was driven by car or rode the bus in Detroit, New York, and Chicago.

Lydia epitomized the woman who, in Gustav's words, finds her "highest worth in humble service and submission."[40] Yet, through her zeal and commitment to the church's ministry as a woman in her own right, she transcended many of the restrictions of her time, even thought of by some as a truly liberated woman. Lydia and her sister Adele Hosto helped to free a segment of North American Protestantism from its own male chauvinism, rediscovering the gifts of women for ministry. Ironically, the deaconess model that Gustav Niebuhr hoped would control and

---

36. *Messenger of Peace*, "Sister Adele Retires."
37. Chrystal, *Father's Mantle*, 79.
38. Reinhold Niebuhr, *Reminiscences of Reinhold Niebuhr*, 5.
39. Reinhold Niebuhr, *Reminiscences of Reinhold Niebuhr*, 6.
40. Chrystal, *Father's Mantle*, 80.

restrict women's freedom in modern society instead opened new vocational doors.

The Niebuhrs brought new life and energy to Lincoln in other ways as well. The Denger family was active in the congregation of St. John before, during, and after the Niebuhrs' tenure there. Florence Denger was a young person in that first decade of a new century, and she later remembered the "fresh air" that blew through Lincoln because of the Niebuhr family and their "new language." Lydia grew up in a bilingual home, and as we have seen, encouraged Gustav in his fluency with English. Both leaned toward the gradual replacement of German with English wherever possible in the life of the congregation. Especially with the young people whose primary language was English, it made no sense to persist in using German. The Niebuhrs used other "new languages" as well. Ms. Denger remembered attending a teachers' meeting in the Niebuhr parsonage during which Lydia suggested an activity for the whole group to undertake, and Gustav "walked across the room and said, 'You can't put everybody in a strait jacket.' That was new language for an Evangelical minister but how refreshing!"[41]

Old pedagogical methods made equal demands for all students, regardless of developmental readiness. Lydia and Gustav worked together as partners in developing new teaching models for ministry. Florence Denger recalled the Niebuhrs' gentle attention to confirmands' individual differences during the traditionally rigid catechism classes. Loving attention and acceptance of learners took precedence over the content of lessons, especially in the case of one "unusually dull and overworked boy" who, according to Denger, responded favorably to the Niebuhrs' sensitivity.[42]

The Niebuhrs faced several stressful challenges during their Lincoln years. In 1906, adding to the already difficult tasks of the pastorate and administration of the hospital, Gustav launched a new quarterly journal. *Der Evangelische Diakonissen-Herold* sought to recruit deaconesses and sow seeds of enthusiasm for the deaconess movement throughout the Evangelical Synod. At about

---

41. Denger, "Letter to Hulda Niebuhr," 1.
42. Denger, "Letter to Hulda Niebuhr ," 2.

the same time, Gustav published a booklet of his views on the "lodge question" in the synod, addressing a controversy long debated in German American communities. In 1907, at the annual conference of the Evangelical Synod which he hosted in Lincoln, Gustav was elected president of the North Illinois District. The tremendous workload of all these tasks resulted in a case of "prostration," an emotional and physical breakdown that prompted St. John Church to grant their pastor a six-month sabbatical in Germany for recuperation. Son Walter had just completed high school. Fifteen-year-old Reinhold would leave for the Elmhurst pre-seminary the following September. After five brief years in Lincoln with the family together, Lydia was again left at home as a single resident parent. Gustav took leave from his many responsibilities, including four teenagers. When Gustav returned from Germany, he went back to his former headlong pace of wider church activity. He became a founding member of the Evangelical Deaconess Association and spoke at its first meeting in September 1908. Two months later he hosted a large ecumenical Protestant Deaconess Conference at St. John. He also helped to establish the first Deaconess Hospital in Chicago.[43]

In 1910 there was much happiness to celebrate in the Niebuhr home. Reinhold graduated from Elmhurst and began his seminary training in St. Louis at Eden. After a year at Illinois Wesleyan, Walter and a friend purchased the Lincoln *Morning Courier* newspaper. As a part of the St. John golden jubilee observance, the congregation also honored their pastor on the twenty-fifth anniversary of his ordination. Two years later, the congregation celebrated the silver wedding anniversary of the Niebuhrs, presenting Lydia and Gustav with a table setting of sterling silverware engraved with the date, May 8, 1912. Also, that year, Helmut graduated from Elmhurst and enrolled at Eden, and Hulda began part-time studies at Lincoln College. Walter added the afternoon *News-Herald* to his local publishing empire in 1912, and the eldest of the Niebuhr boys became president of the *Courier-Herald* company and managing editor of both dailies. Walter's bid to challenge

---

43. Chrystal, *Father's Mantle*, 95–101.

the entrenched Illinois Democratic machine and its thoroughly partisan media included an unsuccessful campaign for Congress in the 1912 Democratic primary. Logan County was decidedly Republican in politics, especially among the German Americans. Walter Niebuhr challenged the old German proverb about the apple not falling far from the tree.[44] But his mother was always very proud of Walter and his accomplishments, no matter how secular or ill fated. She faithfully kept a detailed scrapbook of his career, from high school athletics to the end of his abbreviated lifetime.[45]

The year 1912 also brought great grief to the Niebuhr home and their Hosto kin. The family mourned the loss of E. J. "Papa Hosto." Lydia's beloved father died on September 6, at age seventy-nine, his heart's desire granted, "to die with my boots on."[46] The Evangelical Synod pastor, pioneer, missionary, and church organizer was still active in the parish ministry at the time of his death. He was serving the Ridge Prairie church for the third time when his heart failed and ended his long itinerant ministry. His survivors included his second wife, Philippine; seven of his twelve children; and many grandchildren.[47]

Seven short months later, Lydia's husband succumbed to diabetes. Gustav Niebuhr fell ill during Sunday morning worship on April 13, 1913. That afternoon, a Lincoln physician diagnosed his condition and recommended rest and a strict diet. Instead, the busy pastor worked all weekend and by the following weekend had slipped into a diabetic coma. On Monday, April 21, Gustav Niebuhr died. Only three months before, he had celebrated his fiftieth birthday, what Victor Hugo is said to have called "the youth of old age." Now Lydia, the Niebuhrs and Hostos, St. John Church, the wider Lincoln community, friends of Emmaus Homes and the deaconess movement, and the entire Evangelical Synod were stunned. An elaborate and large funeral marked Pastor Niebuhr's

---

44. Fox, *Reinhold Niebuhr*, 45–47.
45. Carol Niebuhr Buchanan, interview with author, Mar. 17, 1993.
46. Bode, "Pastor Eduard Jakob Hosto," 662.
47. *Lincoln Daily News-Herald*, "Rev. E.J. Hosto Died."

passing. He was buried among the oaks and firs shading Union Cemetery, just outside Lincoln to the south.[48]

At the time of Gustav's death, Reinhold was only weeks away from graduation at Eden Seminary, 150 miles from Lincoln. Approaching his twenty-first birthday, Reinhold returned home to serve his late father's pulpit for the summer. There he rejoined his mother and siblings in the parish and wider community ministries of St. John Evangelical Church. In September Reinhold left Lincoln for Yale Divinity School and more theological study, a move recommended by both his late father and his Eden mentor, seminary president Samuel Press. Helmut then began his second year at Eden, stepping into some of the student-leader roles his brother had so ably filled before him. Walter, as the eldest son and only full-time breadwinner, had a new home built for the family on Union Street in Lincoln, since the parsonage was now to be occupied by Gustav's successor. Hulda and Lydia continued to teach and direct the Sunday school and to work with the hospital and deaconess society but without pay.[49]

Lincoln was still home to the Niebuhrs. Their eleven years there had established them in this place in ways they had never enjoyed in their more itinerant years in California and Missouri. In forty-three peripatetic years, Lydia had never lived so long in any one place. But these local roots were not as deep as her vocation in ministry and her need to be engaged in parish life with members of her family, wherever they might be called to go. Frau Pastor Niebuhr, "the little lady / Who's the spirit of the home,"[50] would be transplanted to equally nourishing soil.

---

48. Chrystal, *Father's Mantle*, 109–12; Gimbel et al., *Story of St. John*, 36.

49. Fox, *Reinhold Niebuhr*, 22. A Sunday school certificate (a copy of which is in the author's possession) signed by Lydia and Hulda and dated Oct. 1915 attests to the women's continued involvement at St John in the two years following Gustav's death.

50. Hulda Niebuhr, in Caldwell, *Mysterious Mantle*, 33.

3

Everywhere in the Church Where She Was Needed

Lydia with Bethel Church friends in Detroit, circa 1930.

Lydia Hosto Niebuhr

BETWEEN 1913 AND 1915, the widowed Lydia Hosto Niebuhr lived in Lincoln, Illinois. Though she lacked a paying career, her "churchly vocation" remained intact as she continued to share her "special gifts for service."[1] Frau Pastor Niebuhr remained active in her many volunteer ministries, playing leading roles in her late husband's congregation and its deaconess society, home and hospital. She further developed her skill for what a parishioner would describe as being "everywhere in the church where she was needed."[2] She also remained the "spirit of the home,"[3] caring for her household as a single mother.[4]

Circumstances forced daughter Hulda to withdraw from her part-time studies at Lincoln College to find income-providing work in addition to her continuing volunteer tasks in the educational program of St. John Evangelical Church. Son Walter was established in work outside the church as president and managing editor of the *Courier-Herald* newspapers in Lincoln. But he, too, remained a part of the family's continuing voluntary work in the parish, serving as church troop scoutmaster and coaching the interchurch youth football and basketball teams initiated by his late father's successor. Reinhold spent two academic years at Yale Divinity School, following his ordination and interim Lincoln pastorate in the summer of 1913. Helmut spent these years completing his seminary training at Eden in St. Louis.[5]

Walter Niebuhr and his newspaper fortunes rose and fell between 1912 and 1915. He built a house for the family in 1913 and lost his job in 1915, suffering the first of several serious business reversals to come. The new house on Union Street had exhausted Gustav's small legacy, and Walter could not carry the family's financial load alone. But his experience in journalism and politics, and his fluency in German, helped Walter to land on his feet as a war correspondent in Europe. Reinhold then assumed the role of

1. Chrystal, *Father's Mantle*, 79.
2. Hurrle, "Letter," para. 11.
3. Hulda Niebuhr, in Caldwell, *Mysterious Mantle*, 33.
4. Bingham, *Courage to Change*, 28–34; Fox, *Reinhold Niebuhr*, 22–44.
5. Gimbel et al., *Story of St. John*, 42.

3

Everywhere in the Church Where She Was Needed

Lydia with Bethel Church friends in Detroit, circa 1930.

Lydia Hosto Niebuhr

BETWEEN 1913 AND 1915, the widowed Lydia Hosto Niebuhr lived in Lincoln, Illinois. Though she lacked a paying career, her "churchly vocation" remained intact as she continued to share her "special gifts for service."[1] Frau Pastor Niebuhr remained active in her many volunteer ministries, playing leading roles in her late husband's congregation and its deaconess society, home and hospital. She further developed her skill for what a parishioner would describe as being "everywhere in the church where she was needed."[2] She also remained the "spirit of the home,"[3] caring for her household as a single mother.[4]

Circumstances forced daughter Hulda to withdraw from her part-time studies at Lincoln College to find income-providing work in addition to her continuing volunteer tasks in the educational program of St. John Evangelical Church. Son Walter was established in work outside the church as president and managing editor of the *Courier-Herald* newspapers in Lincoln. But he, too, remained a part of the family's continuing voluntary work in the parish, serving as church troop scoutmaster and coaching the interchurch youth football and basketball teams initiated by his late father's successor. Reinhold spent two academic years at Yale Divinity School, following his ordination and interim Lincoln pastorate in the summer of 1913. Helmut spent these years completing his seminary training at Eden in St. Louis.[5]

Walter Niebuhr and his newspaper fortunes rose and fell between 1912 and 1915. He built a house for the family in 1913 and lost his job in 1915, suffering the first of several serious business reversals to come. The new house on Union Street had exhausted Gustav's small legacy, and Walter could not carry the family's financial load alone. But his experience in journalism and politics, and his fluency in German, helped Walter to land on his feet as a war correspondent in Europe. Reinhold then assumed the role of

1. Chrystal, *Father's Mantle*, 79.
2. Hurrle, "Letter," para. 11.
3. Hulda Niebuhr, in Caldwell, *Mysterious Mantle*, 33.
4. Bingham, *Courage to Change*, 28–34; Fox, *Reinhold Niebuhr*, 22–44.
5. Gimbel et al., *Story of St. John*, 42.

breadwinner, accepting an assignment to serve a struggling new German Evangelical Synod congregation in Detroit instead of pursuing a PhD.

But biographer Richard Fox puts too much emphasis on this familial economic burden in relation to Reinhold's decision for the pastorate. The Evangelical Synod graduate was obliged to serve in the ministry after a free education at Elmhurst College (pre-seminary) and Eden Seminary. "Elmhurst, Eden, and Eternity" was an educational tradition that cultivated a link between institutional loyalty and heavenly destiny. The call to serve a parish was also in the young theologian's blood. The memory and legacy of Father Niebuhr and Grandfather Hosto cast a long shadow over the entire family. When Reinhold was ordained, just two months after his father's death and nine months after his grandfather's, the young Niebuhr could not have known what the officiating minister had meant when he borrowed the prophetic image of the biblical Elijah story: "We are about to lay the mantle of a father upon the son," a clergy friend of his late father intoned.[6] The mantle proved to represent a father's and grandfather's wanderlust and missionary zeal as much as the call to the Evangelical pulpit. Reinhold and his siblings inherited, from both parents, a familial burden to serve.

Reinhold reported to Bethel Evangelical Church in Detroit in August 1915. Little more than a month later, he was informing the church council that he would be absent from the pulpit on the first Sunday in November, and he had asked his brother Helmut to preach for him.[7] Lydia joined this family ministry after Christmas, bringing stability and security to both unemployed widow mother and unmarried pastor son. She immediately became involved. Frau Pastor Niebuhr appeared in the minutes of the January meeting of the Frauenverein, less than a month following her move from Lincoln to Detroit.[8] By March, she had a committee assignment, and by November her recorded inventory of handmade items for the women's bazaar surpassed all others'.

6. Chrystal, *Father's Mantle*, 111–12.
7. Bethel Church Council, "Minutes," Oct. 15, 1915.
8. Bethel Church Frauenverein, "Minutes," Jan. 1916.

Lydia Hosto Niebuhr

By 1917, Lydia was superintendent of the Sunday school (known also as Bible school) and teacher of the adult class, and she had organized Bethel's first junior choir and was writing most of the monthly *Bethel Bulletin*. By 1918, she had taken over supervision of the home department.[9]

In a 1915 entry in Reinhold's published pastoral diary, the young pastor expressed great relief that his mother was coming to join him to assume responsibility for the organizational life of the parish. "Difficult as the pulpit job is," he admitted, "it is easier than the work in the organizations of the congregation." He acknowledged his mother's natural expertise and his own limits. "Where did anyone learn in a seminary how to conduct or help with a Ladies Aid meeting? I am glad that mother has come to live with me and will take care of that part of the job." Reinhold went on to echo remarks with which he had framed the introduction to *Leaves from the Notebook of a Tamed Cynic*, acknowledging the necessity and challenge of staying at home to do the daily pastoral work vis a vis the prophetic possibilities of an "irresponsible itinerancy." "It is easier to speak sagely from the pulpit than to act wisely in the detailed tasks of the parish." He also established his preference for the prophetic, dependent as his ministry was on the responsible and attentive omnipresence of his middle-aged mother: "A young preacher would do well to be heard more than he is seen."[10]

Christmas, the highest of church holy days among the Germans, had a special meaning in the lives of the Niebuhrs and the congregations they served. They could celebrate the nativity of the Son of God and the wife or mother of their beloved pastor on the same day. Bethel member John Hurrle appreciated the festivity of this coincidence: "I particularly remember one year when Christmas [Lydia's birthday] came on Sunday. She was enthusiastically greeting everyone with a 'Merry Christmas' which only she could give."[11] This exuberance and heartfelt sincerity, combined with her

---

9. See *Bethel Bulletin*, 1915–18.
10. Reinhold Niebuhr, *Leaves from the Notebook*, 2.
11. Hurrle, "Letter," para. 11.

gifts of music and the decorative arts, enhanced other important days of the church year. Reinhold began a 1919 entry in his diary praising his mother for making Bethel appear larger and more attractive than it really was: "We had a great Easter service today. Mother made the little chapel look very pretty, working with a committee of young women. It takes real work to decorate such a little place and make it really inviting."[12] Characteristically, Mother Niebuhr's own account of the same event failed to mention her own role, giving all credit to others: "All decorations for the church at Easter time were made by the girls of the Sunday school. They came together for several weeks and worked most diligently."[13]

Lydia became known almost immediately in 1916 as Bethel's unofficial assistant pastor, the mistress of the manse whose energy and skill touched virtually every aspect of the congregation's life. Caldwell summed up Mother Niebuhr's gift for social reproduction: "Lydia delighted in being with people and enabling them to feel part of a group, a family, a church community."[14] Reinhold did not deny his mother's paraprofessional role but understated it when he later remembered how his hopes had been fulfilled when his mother joined him in Detroit: "My mother . . . was a remarkable person who was kind of an assistant to my grandfather and then to my father, and subsequently to me."[15] Lydia was "kind of" a parish deaconess, too, the woman who attended to the daily rounds of ministry for which the pastor was often ill-suited. "She had great organizational skill," Reinhold wrote. "She made life rather sufferable for me as a young parson who didn't like to do this organizational work."[16] In the dedication of his first book, *Does Civilization Need Religion?*, written while Reinhold and Lydia were in their last year together at Bethel, he memorialized his father, "who taught me that the critical faculty can be united with a reverent spirit," and honored his mother, "who for twelve years

---

12. Reinhold Niebuhr, *Leaves from the Notebook*, 20.
13. L. Niebuhr, "Notes," in *Bethel Bulletin* (Apr. 18, 1919), 4.
14. Caldwell, *Mysterious Mantle*, 31.
15. Bingham, *Courage to Change*, 102.
16. Reinhold Niebuhr, *Leaves from the Notebook*, 2.

has shared with me the work of a Christian pastorate." This may be the clearest and most revealing single statement of the respective legacies of Gustav and Lydia Niebuhr.[17]

For Mother Niebuhr the work of a Christian pastorate meant caring for an ever-widening domestic sphere, housekeeping for her son and their church, whose name in Hebrew means house of God. John Hurrle remembered her reach: "Mrs. Niebuhr was everywhere in the church where she was needed, greeting parishioners and visitors as they came to Sunday school or church services, or taking care of needed items."[18] Lydia became known and cherished for her warm, personal greetings and friendliness, a pastoral touch that "fed the family" of the congregation in socially reproductive and spiritually nourishing ways. Bethel friend Florence Schulz reminisced: "How well I remember my first years in Detroit—when Reinhold Niebuhr and his dear mother Lydia were living on Lothrop Avenue. . . . The whole congregation and the minister and his mother welcomed us with open arms. . . . Being new in town Mother Niebuhr took me under her wing."[19]

Richard Fox characterizes the Sunday school as Lydia's "pet project."[20] Ronald Stone, in a biography that intentionally challenges Fox in many respects, emphasizes Reinhold's lifelong ministry of teaching and links its origins to his mother: "Lydia's piety and emphasis on religious education shaped Reinhold and propelled him toward his vocation."[21] This piety and emphasis shaped and propelled her other children as well. "Shaping" and "propelling" are apt words to describe her vocational mission as exemplified during the Bethel years. Throughout every year from early 1916 through the summer of 1928, she taught an adult or young people's class and also served as either general superintendent or supervisor of teachers in the Sunday school. But this "pet project" had a broader purpose in her vision of ministry.

17. Reinhold Niebuhr, *Does Civilization Need Religion?*, dedication, n.p.
18. Hurrle, "Letter," para. 11.
19. Schulz, "Letter" (1986), 1.
20. Fox, *Reinhold Niebuhr*, 63.
21. Stone, *Professor Reinhold Niebuhr*, 4.

Everywhere in the Church Where She Was Needed

The *Bethel Bulletin* was a monthly newsletter until 1921, when it became a weekly publication that included the Sunday liturgy along with announcements and reports. Evident throughout the *Bulletin* are Lydia's unsigned editorial remarks, consistently revealing her evangelistic and missionary interests. In fact, after 1917 the *Bulletin* appears to be the product of her invisible hand, save for occasional front-page comments from Reinhold. After 1921, the weekly version, filled with promotion and celebration, may be safely attributed to her exclusively. "Every church must depend upon the missionary and evangelistic zeal of its members for its vitality and growth," Lydia asserted in 1923, going on to ask, "Are you a missionary or do you 'just belong'?"[22] The question "What will you do?" and the theme "Be a booster!" ran throughout the newsletters.[23] Bethel's motto for the year 1922, "Every member engaged in some form of Christian service," was always Lydia's goal for the congregation.[24]

By 1918 Lydia's Bible class for women was well attended and filled with enthusiasm, while the Bethel men's class languished. Much *Bulletin* editorial ink spilled over this ongoing problem. Special recruitment efforts focused on the men's class. "How many of our men will be recruited within the next few Sundays?" Lydia wondered in November 1918, seeking to instill some sense of responsibility among Bethel men as role models for their sons: "Where men go, boys will follow. Support the boys, men, by the interest and support which you give our Bible School work." She then sounded the note for lifelong learning, often to be struck: "Incidentally, your Christian education has never been completed. It can never be completed but there are many things you still may learn. Stop learning and you stop growing; stop growing and you stop living. Join the Men's Bible Class."[25]

---

22. Bethel Church bulletin, Dec. 9, 1923.

23. See, e.g., "Be a Booster!," a poem on the back cover, with the invitation for Rally Day and tenth anniversary celebration of Bethel, Bethel Church bulletin, Oct. 8, 1922.

24. Bethel Church, *Retrospect and Prospect*.

25. "Sunday School Notes," in *Bethel Bulletin*, Nov. 1918.

The following year Mother Niebuhr began a promotional contest to award ever-larger attendance in the entire Sunday school, reaching toward an enrollment goal of five hundred students. "The school is going to be divided into two sides," Lydia announced, "the boys and men on one side and the girls and women on the other. A silver loving cup will be presented to the side which maintains the best attendance and secures the largest number of new scholars . . . We're going to have some real fun before this campaign is over."[26]

By 1925 Reinhold could report "the most richly blessed year in the history of our church," when the Sunday school passed the five hundred mark in enrollments and Bethel's superintendents and teachers "earned the recognition of church school leaders in the city" for their faithful and excellent services."[27] Twelve years later, in Bethel's silver anniversary booklet, the congregation continued to savor the honor and boast of the educational leadership dating back to the Niebuhr era.[28] But a larger and better-taught Sunday school was not an end in itself. It was a social and spiritual framework on which to build a solid congregation. "The future of a church is no greater than its Bible school is strong. We need workers and missionaries," Lydia pled in 1922. Much of the growth at Bethel may be attributed to the expanded outreach of the Sunday school. During Lydia's first four years at Bethel, Sunday school enrollment surpassed the number of church members. With her growing army of teachers, officers, and auxiliaries, Lydia enabled the congregation to broaden its ownership of the religious education program. Mother Niebuhr patiently taught all her children that learning prepares members for worship in the church and service for the "wider kingdom of God."[29]

Lydia worked to develop a context for understanding her son's preaching, which, though attractive in its dynamic presentation, sometimes soared over the heads of Bethel churchgoers. "We

26. "Sunday School Notes," in *Bethel Bulletin*, Sept. 1919.
27. "1925 in Retrospect," in Bethel Church, *Bethel Year Book* (1926).
28. Bethel Church, *Brief History*.
29. "Bible School Notes," in Bethel Church bulletin, Oct. 1, 1922.

Everywhere in the Church Where She Was Needed

need Bible versed Christians in our day," she wrote in the newsletter. "The church service assumes your knowledge of the Bible but does not impart it," she explained.[30] For the 1922 Lenten season, Lydia proposed five disciplines to prepare Bethel people for a joyous celebration of Easter: Practice some special self-denial, be a missionary, bring others to church, establish a family altar daily devotion in your home, visit other members of the church, and enlist for service.[31]

Similarly, a 1924 Lenten admonition made it clear that spiritual disciplines were not intended simply for self-improvement. Lydia carried on the pietistic tradition of her father, asking, "Has [sic] your faith and love ever kindled another life into faith and love?" For the Hostos and Niebuhrs, spiritual life, though heartfelt and personal, was never exclusively private or inward. Rather, it was practical, expressive and social. "The vitality of our faith is measured by its missionary power," Lydia wrote. "Be a missionary."[32]

Mother Niebuhr chaired missionary committees in both the women's association and the Evangelical League, and she was a member of the congregation's committee to promote the Evangelical Forward Movement, a synod-wide development campaign launched in 1920. Reinhold served as a synod leader in this "intensive effort to enlist our whole church in our whole task," which was defined in terms of eight objectives: 1) cultivate prayer life, 2) enlist more workers, 3) educate in stewardship, 4) develop religious education, 5) enlarge our colleges, 6) establish new churches, 7) expand foreign missions, and 8) provide for larger pensions.[33] This mission emphasis to "enlist our whole church in our whole task" also characterizes the broader purpose of Lydia Niebuhr's educational ministry. Bethel directly supported an Evangelical Synod missionary in India, Armin Meyer.

---

30. "Sunday School Notes," in Bethel Church bulletin, Sept. 17, 1922.
31. "How to Get Ready for a Great Easter," in Bethel Church bulletin, Mar. 5, 1922.
32. Bethel Church bulletin, Mar. 23, 1924.
33. "The Evangelical Forward Movement," in *Bethel Bulletin* (Sept. 1920) 4.

Lydia Hosto Niebuhr

Lydia connected his work on a foreign mission field to the task of religious education in Detroit: "Help us to train your children in generous giving and particularly for the mission cause. To give regularly for the mission enterprise will help our young people to become world citizens with world sympathies." Such globalism stands in marked contrast to the overwhelmingly isolationist views of many Americans in 1925. Bethel Sunday school offerings often surpassed those of the general membership in support of mission projects beyond Bethel.[34]

Bethel members did not regard Mother Niebuhr as less a minister than her ordained son, who made a flurry of calls on Saturday and preached on Sunday. She did everything else throughout the week when Reinhold was gone. Official resolutions of the council and congregation acknowledged her special vocation within the Bethel fellowship in 1922: "We extend our heartfelt thanks to Mrs. Niebuhr, our pastor's mother, who has selflessly devoted her strength and time to the upbuilding of our Sunday school and church, whose cheerfulness and loving regard for our children is inestimable."[35]

Florence Schulz summed up Lydia's ministry in more personal terms when she wrote, "She was a guiding light to many people. Her smile and a pat on the back was [sic] better than medicine. I gloried in this relationship, and never a day passed before we had a greeting for each other."[36] But her ministry was not simply pastoral encouragement, according to Schulz. "Mother Niebuhr was a 'Go Getter.' In her sweet way she was never turned down. . . . We all loved Reiny and Lydia, his mother! We feel we have been privileged."[37] Hers was a ministry of presence and stability that perfectly complemented her son's itinerant spirit.

34. Bethel Church bulletin, June 14, 1925.

35. Bethel Church Council, "Minutes," Jan. 1922 (annual meeting), 226. This is similar to a resolution passed at the previous year's annual meeting: "To our pastor and his mother who by their remarkable efforts are in good measure responsible for the rapid growth of Bethel Church we extend sincere thanks and appreciation" (Bethel Church Council, "Minutes," Jan. 1921, 168).

36. Schulz, "Letter" (1988), 4.

37. Schulz, "Letter" (1986), 3–4.

Everywhere in the Church Where She Was Needed

According to Bethel's annual report for 1917, Reinhold had spoken twenty-six times in other congregations that year. The 1919 report showed sixty-seven "addresses in other cities" and twenty-two "conferences attended elsewhere." In 1921 the pastor's time away was further broken down as thirty-eight "addresses in city outside congregation," twenty-nine "addresses outside city," and thirty-three "days spent in conferences outside city." A year later Bethel dedicated its new, enlarged building, and the report of the pastor's activities was arranged to show that worship attendance and the numbers of Bethel services, weddings, and "addresses in city" were all up, while the number of addresses and conferences outside the city were reduced by 40 percent. Numbers for 1923 reflected the addition of evening services from autumn through spring, combining with the larger auditorium to make increases in overall worship and Sunday school attendance worth reporting. All categories of Reinhold's extracurricular ventures were then consolidated as 106 "addresses outside church." With such opportunities ever on the increase, it is understandable that after 1924 the annual reports listed only weddings, baptisms, and funerals under "Activities of the Pastor."[38]

Less understandable is the fact that the church council minutes reflect little concern about the pastor's many absences over the years, except for Reinhold's occasional pledge to spend more time at home with Bethel. The greater Reinhold's reputation grew from outside engagements and writing, the more beloved he became as the popular and wise, albeit absent, pastor. As he proposed in his diary, he was doing well by being heard more than seen. This curious fact of a popular preacher's biography is not so much ironic, as Richard Fox suggests, as it is attributable to the depth of the Niebuhr family bench from which Reinhold could call up pinch hitters. Lydia, Hulda, Helmut, and even Walter filled in for Reinhold, and without them, his Bethel pastorate could not have succeeded or endured for thirteen years.[39]

---

38. Bethel Church, *Bethel Year Book*, 1917–24.

39. Fox, *Reinhold Niebuhr*, 62–65. Fox's view does not fully take into account the involvement of the entire Niebuhr clan at Bethel Church, even after

"The whole family served Bethel," as Ronald Stone formulated it, "but Lydia's was the continuous presence."[40] After a long paragraph of praise for Bethel's progress during Reinhold's pastorate, John Hurrle added: "Behind all of these accomplishments there was the day-in, day-out constant support of Lydia Niebuhr!"[41] Observed colleague Ralph Abele, "If there is anything more than another that the people of a congregation long for from the woman of the parsonage, it is firm and quiet strength devoid of ostentation, assurance of understanding, a capacity to see and to help do what most needs doing, be it ever so simple, ever so hard. Mrs. Niebuhr gave the people of Bethel that."[42]

Bethel Evangelical Church grew dramatically during the Niebuhrs' years there. At the end of the "Great War," there were just over one hundred members. By 1922, when the little chapel at the corner of Linwood and Lothrop was replaced with a large new building on West Grand Boulevard, the membership had quadrupled in size. But Bethel's growth, expanded ministry, and new building and Reinhold's ever-increasing itinerancy between weekends required more direction than even Mother Niebuhr and her corps of volunteers could provide. In the summer of 1923, Reinhold joined Sherwood Eddy's "American Seminar" in Europe for ten weeks. This absence demanded a full-time paid assistant pastor for Bethel.[43]

Theodore Braun was called to this ministry in September 1923. Like Niebuhr brothers Reinhold and Helmut, Braun had supplemented his Eden education at Yale. He was a classmate of Helmut and already acquainted with the family when the Evangelical Synod sent him to Detroit, his salary to be paid by Sherwood

---

the war; for example, in the June 1920 *Bulletin* we learn that Helmut and Florence would spend much of their honeymoon in Detroit, when Helmut would preach several times in June and July; and both Hulda and Sister Adele spent the summer at Bethel assisting with vacation Bible school.

40. Stone, *Professor Reinhold Niebuhr*, 40.
41. Hurrle, "Letter," 2.
42. Abele, "Woman Named Lydia," 11.
43. Fox, *Reinhold Niebuhr*, 62, 81, 85.

Everywhere in the Church Where She Was Needed

Eddy. In his old age, Braun recalled his three years at Bethel, during which "Mother Niebuhr . . . who was a very able person, was around most of the time, and was kind of a parish leader, too." In 1924 Braun married, and his Texas bride Viola quickly came under the mothering wing of Lydia Niebuhr as Florence Schulz had. "Mrs. Niebuhr was very friendly and considerate," Braun confessed, "and gave us a lot of help—especially Viola."[44]

With the advent of paid pastoral assistants, Lydia stepped aside from her role as general superintendent to be "supervisor of teachers" in the Sunday school. Following Theodore Braun was Harold "Hap" Pflug, who would later teach religious education at Eden. In 1927, amid rumors that Reinhold would leave Detroit to accept one of the many invitations to "wider fields of usefulness,"[45] Ralph Abele joined the Bethel pastoral staff. He, too, came under the wing and spell of "a woman named Lydia" about whom he would rhapsodize thirty years later in a *United Church Herald* biographical sketch of that name.

> At the tag end of Sunday, after the young people's early evening meeting [which Lydia ran], troop with them over to the parsonage several blocks away, let her draw you into some group games including charades, where her son—if he hasn't taken a night train to fill a speaking appointment at some distant place—is likely to engage in considerable clowning. Here was playful fun, kidding, ribbing and laughter; and no one entered into it with more gusto and enjoyment than the hostess. . . .
>
> Many a time one man's heart danced to hear her rippling laughter. On any day one might see her with flowers or fruit on the way to the hospital or a home to see the sick or just to make a friendly call.[46]

Taking nothing away from Abele, Pflug, or Braun, Mother Niebuhr must be recognized as the chief, though unpaid, assistant

---

44. Braun, "Interview."
45. Reinhold Niebuhr, "Letter of Resignation."
46. Abele, "Woman Named Lydia," 11.

in these Bethel years of Reinhold's itinerant pastorate. Her careful, "maternal" attention to pastoral needs at home freed her son to travel for the sake of the wider mission of the church, just as her domestic management had enabled her husband's itinerancy when their children were young at home. Also, since she was the resident "statesman" minister, her son could afford to sound the prophetic notes that "an irresponsible itinerancy supplies."[47] But in her headlong parish involvement and wide-ranging freedom in the parish, Lydia moved away from her earlier spheres as simply pastor's daughter, wife, or mother. With others to regularly stand in for Reinhold as assistant pastor, Lydia assumed an even broader role. She became the congregation's mother, a matriarch of service beyond the job description of even the most effective assistant minister.

Mother Niebuhr appropriated the model for teaching and leading young women into lives of "consecrated Christian service" as celebrated in popular domestic and devotional literature. In 1924 Lydia favorably reviewed one such book in the pages of *The Evangelical Herald*. *Womanhood in the Making* by Margaret Eggleston offered as a model for teaching ministry the "Christian world mother" who would widen the domestic circle of adolescent girls in her tutelage to include "vocation" as well as "home." Such model teachers, according to Eggleston:

> Understand the psychology of the girl; for to develop Christian attitudes, we must appeal to all the life of the girl.... Preferably their teachers should be mature women, mothers if possible, who feel the presence of God in their own lives; women who have a living, working faith; ... who teach positively ... ; who are more interested in life than in creed; who will be willing to study both lesson and girls; whose life will influence them to give of their own lives for the Master.[48]

According to Eggleston, the highest ideal of a young woman is "that she may eventually become a beautiful Christian mother." Though such a model young woman "may not mother children

---

47. Reinhold Niebuhr, *Leaves from the Notebook*, 2.
48. Eggleston, *Womanhood in the Making*, 107.

of her own . . . she will mother the children of the race. . . . A great teacher or leader needs to have the mother-heart and the motherlove." The author sounded notes of similar tone to those of Mother Niebuhr, promoting expressive activities for character building and learning by experience to enjoy servanthood. "We must learn to feed [adolescent girls'] hunger for activity," Eggleston insisted. "We must help them to grow, to expand their lives and to find pleasure and happiness in serving others."[49]

Mothers' Day at Bethel annually celebrated these themes. Whether the inspiration for this Bethel tradition derives from mother, son, or both is unclear. But it is clear that motherhood, and parenthood more generally, were important models for ministry during the Niebuhrs' Detroit years. The longest unison prayer ever printed in the sparse liturgy accompanying the weekly bulletin's parish news between 1921 and 1928 was "A Prayer for Mothers" for Mothers' Day, May 9, 1926. It thanked God for "the sweet ministries of motherhood in human life" and "the Christly power of sacrifice and redemption in mother love." The prayer echoed other Eggleston themes, asking God to widen the vision of "all the good women who are now bearing the pain and weariness of maternity . . . that they may see themselves not as the mothers of one child only but as the patriot women of their nation who alone can build the better future with fresh and purer life." The prayer concluded with a plea for a renewed dedication "to the ministry of love that this world may become a family of Thy people from which hatred and cruelty is banished as it has long been banished from the family hearth."[50]

Bulletin announcements for the May 11, 1924, evening service at Bethel, after which "Mrs. Niebuhr is also leaving for a vacation," proposed two variant titles for the sermon: "The Mother of a Great Man" and "The Biography of a Great Woman."[51] One wonders who

---

49. Eggleston, *Womanhood in the Making*, xi.

50. "A Prayer for Mothers," in Bethel Church bulletin, May 9, 1926.

51. On the unnumbered liturgy page, in the slot for "Sermon" in "Evening Service," the title is "The Mother of a Great Man"; in the "Notes" opposite the liturgy, the title is given as "The Biography of a Great Mother." Bethel Church

the subject of this Mothers' Day address may have been, and if the different titles for the same presentation represent development or merely ambivalence in Reinhold's thinking on the matter. The unsigned poem "A Prayer," also listed in that week's newsletter, could have been written by Margaret Eggleston or Lydia Niebuhr.

> Lord, give the mothers of the world
> More love to do their part;
> That love which reaches not alone
> The children made by birth their own,
> But every childish heart,
> Wake in their souls true motherhood
> Which aims at universal good.[52]

Beyond the celebrations of motherhood, Lydia frequently promoted Christian parenthood and the home in general as a spiritual seminary for all other societies. After Mothers' Day in 1920, she declared a children's week for Bethel in June. She framed the week's theme in the proverb: "The finest obligation in the world is the responsibility of parents for the training of their children."[53] In January 1926, she urged New Year's resolutions to begin family devotions in the home and "surround the character of grown childhood with the atmosphere of faith, reverence and humility."[54] In June of that year Lydia urged parental scrutiny of moving pictures, asking if it isn't the duty of the home "to supervise this important influence upon the impressionable minds of their children?"[55] She did not mention that her son Walter was in Germany at the time, directing popular films such as *The City of Temptation* and *Venetian Lovers*.[56]

In 1925, "the most richly blessed year in the history of [Bethel] church," the pastor and council implemented the "Parish Plan." The growing congregation was divided into nine geographical

---

bulletin, May 11, 1924.
52. "A Prayer," in Bethel Church bulletin (May 11, 1924) 3.
53. "Sunday School Notes," in *Bethel Bulletin*, June 1920.
54. Bethel Church bulletin, Jan. 3, 1926.
55. Bethel Church bulletin, June 6, 1926.
56. Carol Niebuhr Buchanan, interview with author, Mar. 17, 1993.

districts or neighborhood groups, each of which was presided over by a lay leader. Each "parish" held quarterly or semiannual social meetings to help maintain the friendly "family feeling" in the developing urban church.[57] Lydia's goal of regular visitation to foster a stronger "social spirit" among churchgoers was thus delegated to trained laity. In the fall of 1926, she promoted the Sunday evening service for its model format as a democratic family that demonstrates "the social method of arriving at truth. A real church is not one which hears patiently what the preacher declares to be true, but which initiates a mutual search for truth."[58] An October evening topic, "Can the Family Be Made Democratic?," included questions such as "Is motherhood a profession?" and "Is equality of the sexes achieved only by economic independence of women?" One can imagine Mother Niebuhr's interest in these questions.[59]

Lydia Hosto Niebuhr was a strong woman, and her relationships with her family and church were complex. Hulda regarded her mother as "the little lady / Who's the spirit of the home."[60] We have seen that she was admired in her Lincoln and Detroit congregations. But Reinhold's widow, Ursula, later remembered a quite different "little lady." Ursula (Keppel-Compton) Niebuhr, an Oxford scholar who joined the family after it had moved to the East and shed its Midwestern German American provincialism, never appreciated her mother-in-law as a woman in her own right. To Ursula, Lydia personified a stifling dependence, demeaning of womanhood as she understood it: "[Lydia] herself told me more than once that when her husband died, she did not miss him because Reinhold took his place. She depended on him in every way."[61] Biographer Richard Fox uncritically accepts this one-dimensional perspective and embellishes Ursula's view that Lydia suffered from

---

57. Bethel Church, *Bethel Year Book* (1926).
58. "Notes," in Bethel Church bulletin, Sept. 26, 1926.
59. "Notes," in Bethel Church bulletin, Oct. 17, 1926.
60. Hulda Niebuhr, in Caldwell, *Mysterious Mantle*, 33.
61. U. Niebuhr, "Letter," 1. Ursula's critical evaluation of Lydia is softened in her collection of letters, U. Niebuhr, *Remembering Reinhold Niebuhr*, 408-23.

an excessive, unhealthy dependence on Bethel and Reinhold and thereby restricted her son's maturation as a young man.[62]

No doubt an economic and emotional need did tie her to Reinhold and the church. But the evidence also suggests a mutual dependence. Reinhold needed his mother, and Bethel needed a pastor throughout the week. Lydia thrived on serving and being needed. She, no less than her son, late husband, or father, was driven by a sense of divine calling. Sharing her "mother-heart" and "mother-love" was her vocation.[63] Organizing and directing parish life was her career. One cannot understand the vocation of a living subject's history in strictly psychological or economic terms. To some degree, the biographer must appreciate, or at least evaluate, the validity of the subject on her own terms.

In 1917, shortly after the United States entered the "Great War," the German Evangelical Synod established a War Welfare Commission to oversee pastoral services for the church's young men in the armed forces. Synod president John Baltzer convinced twenty-five-year-old Reinhold Niebuhr to assume the new position of executive secretary of the commission. Baltzer wanted the headquarters to be near the synod offices in St. Louis, but Reinhold was loathe to drag his mother away from Bethel, again dislocating her after only two years in Detroit. Reinhold got his way and the job, retaining his weekend pulpit and doing the synod work throughout the week. Hulda and Helmut joined their mother in assisting at Bethel and helping Reinhold with commission affairs.[64]

Helmut Richard Niebuhr had been ordained in 1916, and for two years served a St. Louis congregation, Walnut Park Evangelical Church. After his first year there, he introduced English-language services and sided with the young people who complained they could not understand the German used in confirmation instruction and worship. Helmut's wish to enter the American mainstream culture and follow his brother Reinhold to Yale Divinity School was postponed for a few years. Instead, he received a master's

62. Fox, *Reinhold Niebuhr*, 173.
63. Terms in Eggleston, *Womanhood in the Making*, xi.
64. Fox, *Reinhold Niebuhr*, 49–61.

degree from Washington University while serving his North St. Louis parish. The tragic drowning death of several church youth under his care left an emotional scar on this the most sensitive of the Niebuhr children.[65] During this St. Louis pastorate, Helmut's friend and Elmhurst-Eden classmate, Eugene "Pat" Baltzer, was killed in an accident while serving his first church in a western state. Helmut's touching poem, "In Memory of My Co-Worker 'Pat,'" reveals something of the temperament that this youngest Niebuhr is said to have inherited from his mother and the Hostos. Note also the romantic subtheme of "the West" as that place where the poet's parents had met and his grandfather had pioneered more than a generation before.

> So Pat's gone West? He always loved the West
> The mountains, forests, cities and the sea;
> He loved the people better, Christ the best
> And went to work there on the symphony
> Of God and man and nature, faithfully.
>
> For he was one who ever sought the way
> Of harmony. Remember how he bent
> His head down to his fiddle, felt the play
> Of bow and string vibrate through his intent,
> Sensitive hand till soul with music blent?
>
> He was that sort of man, harmonious, pure;
> A world like that he wanted, under God,
> The Great Symphonist; so he went to endure,
> To do what one man could. He trod
> A lonesome way sometimes, except for God.
>
> Don't say he's dead; he's sunset bound again
> Out past the Gate, to Islands of the Blest;
> To work with Christ, to play a grander strain,
> To climb clean-handed and with the cleaner breast
> The hills of heaven in a holier West.[66]

---

65. Diefenthaler, *H. Richard Niebuhr*.
66. H. Richard Niebuhr, "In Memory."

Lydia Hosto Niebuhr

In 1918 the late "Pat" Baltzer's synod-president father suggested that Helmut replace Reinhold as Bethel's pastor, given the elder Niebuhr brother's outside commitments and interests and Helmut's frequent trips to Detroit to fill the Bethel pulpit.[67] Instead, Helmut accepted the call to join the Eden Seminary faculty, fulfilling a dream his own father had had on his way home from Utah in 1902.[68] Also, in 1918 sister Hulda left Detroit as her permanent residence, and for the next ten years studied and taught at the Boston University School of Religious Education and Social Service. Hulda created something of a tradition for Evangelical Synod women seeking a theoretical grounding for their parish work in religious education. (There were no women's colleges in the synod until 1930.)[69] Hulda also wrote experimental curricula while at Boston, sending them home to mother at Bethel for testing.[70]

In June 1920, Helmut married Florence Mittendorf, a daughter of the Lincoln congregation, with brother Reinhold officiating at St. John Church there.[71] On September 23, brother Walter also married, but under rather different circumstances. Since his own departure from Lincoln, Walter had lived in Europe and Mexico, and evolved from print journalism to writing, directing, and producing plays and motion pictures. Instead of "going home" to find and wed a bride, Walter married a young actress associated with the Ziegfeld Follies in New York, Beulah Bennett Johnstone.[72] Mother Niebuhr welcomed Beulah into the family without reservation, and after the wedding, the young couple returned to Europe, where they would spend most of the next decade. In 1924, Helmut became the first and only member of the family to earn a doctorate, receiving a PhD from Yale. In that same year, against his better judgment but with the strong encouragement of synod president Baltzer, the thirty-year-old Helmut Richard Niebuhr

67. Fox, *Reinhold Niebuhr*, 60–61.
68. Diefenthaler, *H. Richard Niebuhr*, ix, 6.
69. Caldwell, *Mysterious Mantle*, 27–48.
70. Schulz, "Letter" (1986).
71. "Notes," in *Bethel Bulletin*, June 1920.
72. "Notes," in *Bethel Bulletin*, Oct. 1920.

became president of Elmhurst College. During his three years in this position, the small denominational men's college made significant gains in entering the American academic and cultural mainstream. But this institutional progress was not achieved without taking a serious personal toll on the young Niebuhr, and in 1927 he returned to the faculty of Eden.[73]

During and after the First World War the three Niebuhr brothers were actively seeking to broaden the cultural horizons and challenge the patriotism of their fellow German Americans in general and the German Evangelical Synod of North America in particular. Walter became staunchly pro-American after a few months of eyewitness work covering the war in 1915. In 1916 he produced the "first official American war film" while serving in the army with General Pershing on the Mexican border. In 1917 Walter Niebuhr was appointed to direct the film division of President Wilson's new Committee on Public Information, known as the George Creel Committee. Despite his service record and prolific production of effective motion picture propaganda, the eldest Niebuhr brother was accused of being a "Kaiserite," and the resulting storm of controversy led to his resignation in 1918. "Big Brother Sylvest" was a role model for his younger brothers, both of whom felt the injustice of this incident and thereafter increased their efforts to distance themselves from their German roots.[74]

Reinhold used his "bully pulpit" on the Evangelical Synod's War Welfare Commission to encourage synod congregations to abandon their German sympathies and support the Allied crusade against Germany in both Europe and the United States. In 1918 he urged that "German" be dropped from the Evangelical Synod's name and that the language of his own congregation's worship be changed to English. Helmut, heir of his mother's aesthetic sensibilities and quiet, irenic manner, composed stridently patriotic verses for distribution among soldiers and in congregations, and in 1918 enlisted in the army, though the war ended before he could serve.[75]

73. Diefenthaler, *H. Richard Niebuhr*, 10–17.
74. Chrystal, "'American' without Any 'If,'" 7.
75. Fox, *Reinhold Niebuhr*, 41–61.

Just before that, after a trip through the training camps, Reinhold wrote in his diary with typical realism of the ethical dilemma he and his brother faced.

> What makes me angry is the way I kowtow to the chaplains as I visit the various camps.... It is the uniform and not the cross which impresses me and others.... Helmut is right. He tells me that he wants to go into the army as a private and not as a chaplain. He believes that the war is inevitable but he is not inclined to reconcile its necessities with the Christian ethic. He will merely forget about this difficulty during the war. That is much more honest than what I am doing.[76]

Before the US involvement in the war, Reinhold wrote his first article to be published outside the synod, "The Failure of German-Americanism," in *The Atlantic*. After the war, in his role as a member of the board that oversaw the educational work of the synod, he headed the committee that built a library at Elmhurst as a memorial to the evangelical men who lost their lives as soldiers fighting the Germans. If there was any doubt about the family's loyalties in relation to their status as "hyphenated Americans" before the war, there could be none after. In the words of Walter after his January 1916 return from Europe, where he witnessed the fall of Warsaw and the costly battles of Verdun, Kemmel Ridge, and the Goritzian Bridgehead, "I came home an American citizen—first, last and all the time."[77]

After the war, with Hulda in Boston, Walter in New York, Helmut in St. Louis, and Reinhold freed from his synod work, Mother Niebuhr directed new energies toward the growing Bethel educational program in Detroit. She expanded the Sunday school to include "week-day activities." She addressed the subject for the second national convention of Evangelical Sunday schools, held in Chicago in 1919. Under her direction, Bethel church opened its doors daily after school and work, providing "healthful, life-building . . . channels for self-expression." Religious education

---

76. Reinhold Niebuhr, *Leaves from the Notebook*, 15–16.
77. Chrystal, "'American' without Any 'If,'" 4.

should be practical, Lydia believed. There could be "no impression without expression." "Week-day activities" were not simply intended to fill time for idle hands, but to shape behavior in ways that put Christian principles into practice, "that their characters are strengthened and their ideas so fixed that they will be more able to live the Christian life under all circumstances."[78]

But her address went beyond a description of a successful program she developed at Bethel Church. Her wider audience provided Lydia with a rare opportunity to spell out broader, more general theoretical purposes for the vocation of a religious educator. She offered five basic purposes:

1. To teach "service, love, helpfulness, co-operation." She cautioned that the "greatest danger of religious education is [that] of teaching vague ideals, general truths, in words and examples which are so broad and loose that they have no real meaning for the pupil."

2. To foster "social spirit.... We can never be successful teachers unless we love those whom we teach, have a genuine understanding of their characters, their capabilities, their difficulties and their fine qualities. We do not learn to know them in visits or in Sunday morning hours, but when we work with them and allow them to be their natural, unfettered selves."

3. To help shape their behavior with "a kind of practical experience" that puts Christian principles into practice.

4. To encourage and enable the participant to "share in the ownership of the concern." This purpose, akin to the second, revealed Lydia Niebuhr's capacity to identify with children and youth and her abhorrence of condescension.

5. To welcome newcomers and "bring strangers into connections with the school and with the church." Lydia was always the liberal evangelical missionary.[79]

---

78. Caldwell, *Mysterious Mantle*, 104.
79. L. Niebuhr, "Week-Day Activities," 131–32.

Lydia Hosto Niebuhr

Four years later, relieved of some of her demanding day-to-day parish responsibilities by assistant pastor Theodore Braun's presence at Bethel, Mother Niebuhr stepped into a different kind of promotional role. Now she was not merely encouraging religious educators to expand their outreach in parish settings, but she was addressing the broader educational needs of women in the patriarchal Evangelical Synod. She spoke to the second national convention of the Evangelical Women's Union, a synod-wide organization begun in 1921 to provide support and structure for local church women's groups. Lydia promoted a new kind of home missions enterprise for her denomination, the Oakwood Institute, a "Training School for Service" to open in Cincinnati, Ohio, in 1923. She portrayed the new evangelical institution as a lay women's version of the deaconess movement in which she, her late husband, and Sister Adele Hosto had long been active.[80]

Lydia advanced the notion that women in the Evangelical Synod lacked "opportunity for training in the service which they might have given, and our church has lacked the benefits it might have derived from such trained help."[81] The large Women's Union assembly gathered on the campus of Elmhurst College, then still the exclusively male institution it had been when Reinhold and Helmut attended while sister Hulda stayed at home in Lincoln to teach parochial school. The irony of this was that Elmhurst had long been a place to train young men to be parochial schoolteachers as well as a pre-seminary. Lydia began her address by referring to this inequity. She observed that Elmhurst had long been a place for "sons of our church" to be trained for leadership. Now was the time for the "daughters of our church" to have the same access to training for service.[82]

A year later, son Helmut began his Elmhurst presidency, which introduced a number of Americanizing reforms to upgrade the academic quality of the as-yet-unaccredited synod institution. President Niebuhr would also pave the way for coeducation at

---

80. L. Niebuhr, "Training School for Service."
81. L. Niebuhr, "Training School for Service," 92.
82. L. Niebuhr, "Training School for Service," 92.

Elmhurst, an innovation that began shortly after his return to the Eden Seminary faculty.[83]

In the meantime, son Reinhold's patron and European tour companion, Sherwood Eddy, was luring the rising itinerant star from Detroit. Eddy had paid Theodore Braun's salary at Bethel and in other ways courted Reinhold and cultivated his favor to come to New York. Finally, in April 1928, Eddy succeeded. Reinhold agreed to accept the call to teach at the interdenominational Union Theological Seminary and edit the pacifist monthly journal *The World Tomorrow*. Sherwood Eddy would now pay Niebuhr's salary for the magazine and his newly created seminary position. *The Detroit News* put the story of the Bethel pastor's departure on its front page the Monday following the shocking but not surprising Sunday announcement. On Tuesday the daily's editorial writer said that Niebuhr was leaving "after having built up one of the city's great churches."[84]

The editor told only half the story. As Richard Fox put it, Mother Niebuhr "was the essential material foundation for [Reinhold's] public career."[85] Together, Lydia and Reinhold had built up one of the city's great churches. The Bethel people knew this, even if the newspaper did not, and when the freshman New Yorkers returned to Detroit later in the fall for a proper show of appreciation, the event was clearly directed to "Rev. Niebuhr and His Mother." "The people of Bethel," read the printed program, "affectionately acknowledge not only the invaluable service of Mr. Niebuhr to the life and growth of the church, but also the unselfish and loving devotion of his mother, Mrs. Niebuhr, whose untiring efforts have ever been for the welfare of Bethel."[86]

Mother Niebuhr and her son left the Detroit parish in sound shape. In their tenure, the membership and Sunday school enrollment had increased tenfold. They had built an impressive new building. For Reinhold the move to seminary teaching and

---

83. Crocco, "President H. Richard Niebuhr."
84. Fox, *Reinhold Niebuhr*, 106.
85. Fox, *Reinhold Niebuhr*, 69.
86. Bethel Church, "Farewell Tribute."

Lydia Hosto Niebuhr

journalism outside the Evangelical Synod was an opportunity suited to his ecumenical interests and long-standing struggle with the conservatives in his own denomination who feared losing the baby of their unique theological tradition with the bathwater of the German heritage. "It offers me a field of usefulness so much in harmony with my own inclination that I feel compelled to accept it," he wrote in his letter of resignation. But he also admitted to the great difficulty in his decision, "because my going will rob the congregation of mother's services and I know that whatever success we have had has in a large measure been due to her work in the church."[87]

Reinhold did not realize that his mother was also being robbed of something irreplaceable. For Lydia the move from Detroit to New York meant saying goodbye to every field of usefulness and service for which she had been trained and in which she had had such experience and success. Unlike her rather gentle and easy transplanting from Lincoln to Detroit twelve years before, this move meant a radical and violent uprooting from her vocation as well as location. Nonetheless, she said her sad farewells at Bethel and willingly accompanied her son to Manhattan in time for the fall semester of classes to begin at Union.[88]

---

87. Reinhold Niebuhr, "Letter of Resignation."
88. Fox, *Reinhold Niebuhr*, 111–18.

4

Life Need Never Be Sad or Lonely

Lydia with daughter Hulda at one of their Chicago "wheel parades" with children at the McCormick Theological Seminary campus, Chalmers Place, in the late 1940s.

Lydia Hosto Niebuhr

CLARA HOSTO HAD DIED at age sixty-two in rural southern Illinois. When her daughter Lydia reached that age thirty years later, she was only beginning an entirely new life in New York. In 1928 Lydia had left behind the Evangelical Synod, friends in Detroit and Lincoln, and the busy parish life she had known. Housekeeping for son Reinhold, the Union Seminary professor and pacifist editor, was not enough. The rest of her family was dispersed: Walter and Beulah, while living in Europe, had adopted a daughter, Carol Lydia. They did not return to the states until 1930. Helmut, Florence, and their two children, Cynthia and Richard, lived in St. Louis in 1928 and 1929, and in Europe in 1930. Although Mother was glad to have daughter Hulda move from Boston to Columbia University in New York in 1928, the first years in New York were difficult for the family matriarch. As Hulda's biographer put it, "Essential to [Lydia's] emotional health was purpose in life. She gained her meaning through the lives and careers of her family members."[1] But she had also derived meaning and purpose through engagement with a wider family of teachers, students, and other associates in the parish and denomination that had shaped her and helped to nurture her family.

In her first years in New York, Lydia found herself cut off from the parish deaconess vocation, "extending and promoting the spiritual welfare" and "administering the charities of the church" as an acknowledged and thereby authorized servant of Christ.[2] Mother Niebuhr had no community in which to exercise her vocation. Unlike the interim between Gustav's death in Lincoln and her migration to Bethel in Detroit, this period involved no social or spiritual outlet, no ministry for Lydia's energies and skills. Other than hosting weekly "at homes" in the Niebuhr apartment for Reinhold's students, Lydia had little apparent connection to Union. What she did have certainly did not take the place of the congregational life she had known. She was lost. Yet, in a letter to Detroit, Lydia put the best possible face on her situation in order to encourage a friend. "One's life need never be sad or lonely for

---

1. Caldwell, *Mysterious Mantle*, 31.
2. Gimbel et al., *Story of St. John*, 35.

Life Need Never Be Sad or Lonely

there is so much in the world to make one happy.... Many people of sixty feel life is over. That is often because they have lost interest in others or are blind to the possibilities of this world."[3]

Lydia Hosto Niebuhr was too young to retire at age sixty. But there was a personal crisis of identity and meaning that momentarily blinded her from seeing "the possibilities of this world." Another woman came into her unmarried son's life. The apparently confirmed bachelor professor, thirty-eight years old, met a young and attractive English graduate student from Oxford. Ursula Keppel-Compton came to Union on a graduate fellowship for the 1930–31 academic year. She returned to England the following summer engaged to marry Professor Niebuhr. But their wedding could not be until Reinhold had taught summer school, spoken at many conferences, worked on the manuscript of *Moral Man and Immoral Society*, and completed another fall semester of courses at Union. There was also the matter of Mother Niebuhr, a fixture and given of Reinhold's household for sixteen years. Lydia and her son assumed that Ursula would simply join them. Ursula insisted that Mother Niebuhr must go. After a power struggle during which the engagement was nearly broken off, Ursula emerged the winner, and Lydia moved in with daughter Hulda instead. The December 1931 wedding in England lacked family witnesses on the Niebuhr side. A long vacation and sabbatical in 1930 had exhausted financial resources for the rest of the family. But their absence from the Winchester Cathedral ceremony also "fittingly symbolized," as Richard Fox put it, "the severe break the marriage signified."[4]

This symbolic break opened Mother Niebuhr's eyes to new possibilities, though her relationship to her daughter-in-law was never unreservedly warm. Walter's daughter Carol remembered as a young child sitting between Lydia and Ursula and feeling "arrows of hostility" darting back and forth. Carol says the two women could not be together in the same room without creating palpable

---

3. Eisen, "Letter," 1, quoting from letter from Lydia Niebuhr to Marguerite Eisen; Lydia probably wrote shortly after her honorary degree from Lindenwood College in 1953.

4. Fox, *Reinhold Niebuhr*, 131.

tension.⁵ After all, as Richard Fox analyzed Reinhold's marriage and his mother's exodus: "He was not just leaving his childhood home; for Lydia at least it was abandonment, if not desertion, divorce and remarriage."⁶ But Lydia Hosto Niebuhr was by nature neither unforgiving nor resistant to change. She, too, inherited the family wisdom Helmut would later articulate to encourage his brother to accept an offer for a new position: "Transplantation often helps us to grow."⁷ After Reinhold's wedding, Mother Niebuhr again thrived in a new household and liberating new coworker relationship in a reconfigured parish ministry as her daughter's assistant.

Hulda was doing further graduate work at Columbia University in 1930 when she became associate director of religious education at the large and prestigious Madison Avenue Presbyterian Church. There, Lydia gladly returned to congregational life and at least a portion of the vocation for which she was trained in a lifetime's experience. Though their shared Riverside Drive apartment was not a parsonage or manse, the Niebuhr women were once again together in parish family life, reforming the powerful team of teaching "sisters" they had been in Lincoln and Detroit. At age sixty, coming to be known by her grandchildren as Mütterchen (German term of endearment for an old woman), Lydia for the first time enjoyed the vocational luxury of specialization. She focused her energies and attention on teaching and befriending urban youth. Mütterchen became a surrogate grandmother to poor adolescent girls of junior high school age from Manhattan's East Side.⁸

"Most of her pupils were from the overcrowded homes of the east side," wrote Ralph Abele of Mütterchen's new role, really but an adaptation of the "week-day activities" she had initiated in Detroit and about which she had spoken at the 1919 Chicago Sunday school convention. "Some of the most important lessons of their young lives were learned in the Niebuhr mother-and-daughter

---

5. Carol Niebuhr Buchanan, interview with author, Mar. 17, 1993.
6. Fox, *Reinhold Niebuhr*, 131.
7. H. Richard Niebuhr, "Letter to Reinhold Niebuhr," para. 3.
8. Caldwell, *Mysterious Mantle*, 51–77.

apartment. Sunday luncheons, which girls helped prepare and serve, occasional slumber parties, hobby sessions were all part of the curriculum."[9]

Hulda later described her mother's transplanted ministry in terms of close, personal relationships developed and maintained over time: "In New York Mother taught . . . for about fifteen years. . . . She still receives mail regularly from youngsters who were in her classes then. . . . Any trips of mine out of the city were signal for a looked-for slumber party—then there was room in the apartment for more girls."[10] Mütterchen could once again direct her "mother-heart" and "mother-love" to what Margaret Eggleston had called "womanhood in the making."[11]

Before this creative reunion of the Niebuhr family women, at about the same time that Lydia was suffering her vocational exile, Hulda was hospitalized. Caldwell says Hulda's problem was either chronic back pain (from which she suffered most of her life) or disabling depression. History of emotional disorder in the family suggests the latter. Father Gustav had had his six-month "prostration" and subsequent European "sabbatical" in 1907. The Hostos had their share of mental distress. Walter Niebuhr wrestled with alcoholism. Helmut, while serving as president of Elmhurst College (1924–27), was known to have serious annual spring bouts of "nervous exhaustion" requiring treatment and retreat; and, in 1944, when he reached the age at which his father had died, Helmut was hospitalized for severe depression.[12] After Reinhold's strokes in 1952, he also fought periods of emotional disability. The entire family was "inclined to introversion," as Helmut once put it in a letter to Reinhold, and "it wasn't a good plan to introspect too much when we got into some psychical difficulty."[13] This perceptive analysis came from the most introspective of the Niebuhr

9. Abele, "Woman Named Lydia," 11.
10. Hulda Niebuhr, "Letter to Theodore Braun" (Jan. 31, 1959), para. 3.
11. Eggleston, *Womanhood in the Making*, xi.
12. Fowler, *To See the Kingdom*, 5.
13. H. Richard Niebuhr, Feb. 14, 1930, cited in Fox, *Reinhold Niebuhr*, 121; and in Caldwell, *Mysterious Mantle*, 57.

children, who advised sister Hulda in 1929 "to get busy with something external, preferably something manual," because in his experience, psychotherapy uncovered more problems than could be solved "save by moral victory."[14]

This was certainly the lesson all the children had learned from their mother, whose therapeutic quilts, knitting, embroidery, hooked-rag rugs, hat designing, handsewn draperies and wardrobes for herself and Hulda, doll clothing for her own and others' grandchildren, and other manual projects had seen her through the temptation to "introspect too much" during periods of "psychical difficulty." It was, in fact, during Mütterchen's own unhappy season of apparent uselessness in New York that son Walter returned from his European filmmaking and gave his mother a movie camera. By the time she joined her daughter's teaching ministry at Madison Avenue Presbyterian Church, Mother Niebuhr was on her way to becoming an accomplished amateur photographer. She became very "busy with something external . . . something manual," traveling all over New York City with her movie and still cameras and developing her own still photos in a makeshift apartment closet darkroom.[15] Her movie projector went with her on the bus as she entertained church, school, and other social groups with homemade silent documentaries such as *Children and Their Pets* or dramatic illustrations of children's poems and prayers such as "Thank You for the World So Sweet" and Joyce Kilmer's "Trees." One of her films, *Nature Round*, celebrated the love of nature she learned from her father by portraying the moods of the natural world and activities of children in each of the four seasons. *Our Helpers* reflected her own sense of vocation by showing the postal letter carrier, milk deliveryman, firefighter, and others at their daily rounds. *Sidewalks of New York* was based on the Jane Addams's book *How the Other Half Lives*, revealing life in the tenements. Christmas gifts to her grandchildren included her home movie highlights of the year, capturing their antics at play and while vacationing together with

---

14. Fox, *Reinhold Niebuhr*, 121; Caldwell, *Mysterious Mantle*, 56–57.
15. Carol Niebuhr Buchanan, interview with author, Mar. 17, 1993.

Life Need Never Be Sad or Lonely

family, and featuring her firsthand coverage of the annual Macy's Thanksgiving Day parade.[16]

Mütterchen had a keen photographer's eye and enjoyed taking pictures of Helmut's daughter Cynthia and son Richard, Walter's daughter Carol Lydia, and Reinhold's son Christopher and daughter Elisabeth. Her still, black-and-white snapshots captured her subjects enjoying outdoor activities and nature, whether it was smelling a flower, feeding pigeons in Central Park, enjoying animals at the zoo or sitting on the lawn with a puppy in the afternoon sunshine. When the family began spending summers together in the Berkshire Mountains of western Massachusetts, Mütterchen's cameras came along. She also began collecting ferns and seashells, which were carefully identified, displayed, labelled, and presented in her programs for children and senior citizens. Her collection of sixty-five species of ferns came from summers in the Berkshires as well as other expeditions with family to the Adirondacks and Blue Ridge Mountains. She grew ferns as well, feeding them with a special fertilizer of water drained from cooking calf liver. Her lush ferns were among many other plants and flowers, growing inside and outside, wherever she lived. In warm weather, Lydia was always known to have a large pot of zinnias at her front door. Her seashell collection of more than six hundred pieces began as a child's response to a gift of handsewn doll clothing from Mütterchen. "The child wanted to do something in return," wrote Detroit friend Marguerite Eisen, "so while on vacation at the seaside she collected shells and sent them to Mrs. Niebuhr. Fascinated by the lovely shells, Mrs. Niebuhr became interested and began to classify them."[17] Family and friends received welcome Mütterchen-made gifts of colorful art glass "suncatchers," lanterns and small windows and "Mütterchen blue" hand-printed note cards as greetings at Christmas, a birthday, anniversary, or other occasion. Photography, reading, and these handcraft hobbies combined with five

---

16. Inventory of Lydia Niebuhr films in Eden Theological Seminary archives, Saint Louis; and in St. John United Church of Christ, Lincoln, Illinois.

17. Eisen, "Letter," 2.

loving grandchildren to brighten Mütterchen's prospects for happiness in New York after Reinhold's marriage in 1931.

"She was forward looking," granddaughter Carol remembered. "It was always forward motion with her" and "useless to get her to talk about her past."[18] There was less reason to look back, too, since her family was reconvening from its brief diaspora. By 1931, the Niebuhrs' organizing center had shifted decidedly eastward. The transplanted Midwestern family had regathered within the wingspan of the "mother hen." Walter had returned from Europe and was now an executive and partner in his own New York–based company, Beacon Films. When Helmut became a Yale professor and his family moved to Connecticut, in 1931, the migration was complete. In October, before Reinhold's December wedding in England, the prospective groom wrote to Ursula: "Helmut and his family have arrived and the house is full of Niebuhrs as Walter's wife and child also came. They are all very anxious to meet you."[19] After the wedding and the newlyweds' return from abroad early in 1932, four households of Niebuhrs lived within two hours of one another: Mütterchen and Hulda, and Reinhold and Ursula only blocks apart in Manhattan; Walter, Beulah, and Carol in nearby suburban Tuckahoe, Westchester County; and Helmut, Florence, and their two children in Hamden, Connecticut. Left behind for Mütterchen and the family were Lincoln, Detroit, St. Louis, Elmhurst College, Eden Seminary, the Evangelical Synod, and many of their Midwestern ethnic ties.

Symbolic of this familial and cultural shift, and with the strong encouragement of Florence, Helmut dropped his Germanic first name and came to be known around Yale as Richard. As an author he was H. Richard Niebuhr. Just before his move from Eden to Yale, he had spent a sabbatical in Europe, where he observed the alarming rise of Hitler in Germany and fascism in general. Old battles with conservative Evangelical Synod hard-liners during his St. Louis pastorate, the war, and his years at Elmhurst and Eden had

18. Carol Niebuhr Buchanan, interview with author, Mar. 17, 1993.

19. Reinhold Niebuhr to Ursula Keppel-Compton, Oct. 16, 1931, in U. Niebuhr, *Remembering Reinhold Niebuhr*, 53–54.

complicated the question of his cultural identity while enhancing the appeal of Yale Divinity School's thoroughly American and ecumenical possibilities. Synod leaders such as John Baltzer and the Niebuhr brothers' Eden mentor, Samuel Press, had nurtured seeds of a more Americanized ecumenicity that their liberal parents had planted in their minds.[20] The First World War and the nationalist Nazi perversion of German patriotism and ethnic pride in the decade following caused the Niebuhrs to cut off ties with German cousins, some of whom they had visited as late as 1930. These developments also convinced the Niebuhr family to draw necessary distinctions between religious and national loyalties. H. Richard and Reinhold condemned the so-called "German Christians" for their uncritical accommodation to their culture and capitulation to the ideology of National Socialism. They also praised the small Confessing Church for its courageous withdrawal from the prevailing Zeitgeist.[21] Walter Niebuhr spent 1933 and 1934 producing, directing, and lecturing on two cinematic projects for the Peace Films Foundation, *Must War Be?* and *WHY?*[22] Once again, there could be no question about divided loyalties for this German American family, again affirming Walter's words from an earlier American buildup for war with Germany: "American citizen—first, last and all the time."[23]

Theodore Braun suggested an even longer social history for Helmut Richard Niebuhr's personal struggle with his cultural identity. In Niebuhr's obituary, Braun wrote, "Niebuhr was not fond of his first name. On one occasion, half playfully but also half in earnest, he chided his mother for calling him Helmut, a name that was sometimes ridiculed by persons who did not know German. 'But it is such a beautiful name,' she replied, 'rich in tradition and meaning. Heroic courage is what it means,' she reminded him."[24] Heroic and courageous or not, at the age of thirty-seven, Helmut

20. Chrystal, "Samuel D. Press," 512–13.
21. Diefenthaler, *H. Richard Niebuhr*, 29–30.
22. Carol Niebuhr Buchanan, interview with author, Mar. 17, 1993.
23. Chrystal, "'American' without Any 'If,'" 4.
24. Braun, "In Memoriam."

Richard signaled the end of a personal era and its struggles. Yet, old friends continued to know him as Helmut, and his family retained their version from his childhood, "Hem," and so he signed his most personal correspondence to them.

But it was something more than a merely symbolic end of an era, the persistence of old habits notwithstanding. "Mother church" and "mother tongue" could no longer contain the Niebuhrs. H. Richard had chaired his denomination's Committee on Relations with Other Churches since 1927, the year "German" was finally dropped from the name of the Evangelical Synod of North America. He and Reinhold had agreed that their theological heritage of irenic unionism favored further unity with Reformed rather than confessional Lutheran groups. The Lutherans were more likely to ignore the world around them, they believed, clinging to culture-bound old ways and language. A 1929 Plan of Union proposed to bring together the Evangelical Synod with the United Brethren and the German Reformed Church in a new "United Church of America." When the United Brethren withdrew from the proposed union, however, H. Richard lost heart and thereafter contributed little to the continuing process that resulted in the Evangelical and Reformed Church in 1934. But his disheartening experience did contribute positively to the passionate scholar's interest in writing *The Social Sources of Denominationalism*, a stinging rebuke of a Christendom in North America that was organized according to race and class rather than theological or spiritual principle.[25]

Also in 1929, John Baltzer retired from the presidency of the Evangelical Synod, a watershed moment in the church's history, as he put it in his farewell address:

> Since 1921, the keel of our synodical ship steered straight forward in a course that was necessary for her to take. Her leaders recognized that, if we would continue as a church, our course must now steer forward unconcerned as to language or lineage. We knew it must be our duty to hold the growing generation that knew little or nothing about the German language, the German heritage of our

---

25. Diefenthaler, *H. Richard Niebuhr*, 13–18.

parents and our own.... And today, for the first time in the history of the Evangelical Synod of North America, the president of the Synod reads his report to the General Conference in the language of the country.[26]

Replacing the spoken and written German language in official reports, newsletters, sermons, hymns, prayers, parish teaching and visitation, governing council proceedings, fellowship, choral music, and devotional literature amounted to a cultural revolution of no small proportions. Even the more symbolic changes, such as eliminating the name "German" from the Evangelical Synod and "Helmut" from Richard Niebuhr, signify deeply profound historical shifts that go to the very heart of religious conviction and community identity. Language is, after all, not only the product of a community, as Karl Marx is said to have observed, but it is integrally tied to the very existence of a community. German Americans feared the loss of their language would mean the loss of their culture as well.[27]

Before the First World War, more than 10 percent of the population in the United States was German speaking, and nearly a third of non-English speakers used the German language.[28] More than half of the non-English daily and weekly newspapers were German. The cultural chauvinists of this strong language community, whether Evangelical, Lutheran, Reformed, Methodist, Baptist, Mennonite, Roman Catholic, or anti-church "free thinkers," believed "the German spirit will heal the world."[29] Even the idea of an American "melting pot" may be traced to a German, Christian Essellen, who in 1857 proposed a *Schmeltztiegel* as a way of flavoring an otherwise unsavory ethnic stew.[30] American

26. Dunn et al., *Evangelical and Reformed Church*, 275.

27. Wolf, "Hyphenated America," 1:69: "The strong synthesis between language and ethnic identification was matched by an equally strong tie of both to religion. To belong to a church was to accept its cultural orientation along with its doctrines."

28. Eichoff, "German Language in America," 1:224.

29. Eichoff, "German Language in America," 1:239.

30. Conzen, "German-Americans," 1:133.

church history pioneer Philip Schaff expressed similar views about a special German mission to improve American spirituality and culture. In the arrogant words of the American-born president of a powerful prewar German American organization subsidized by wealthy brewers, "no one will ever find us prepared to step down to a lesser Kultur; no, we have made it our aim to draw the other up to us."[31]

Reinhold Niebuhr's 1916 classic article condemning the "failure of German-Americanism" drew on these same cultural assumptions, to which, of course, language was inextricably tied. When English-speaking Americans chided or shunned their German-speaking neighbors during the war, it was because of the threatening and strident utterances of otherwise loyal Americans. The crushing defeat of Germany had far-reaching cultural consequences in North America. Forces at work since the "nationalist nineties" climaxed in the aftermath of the "Great War." Ethnographer Heinz Kloss says the near extinction of the German language in America reflects the largest assimilation process ever of a single speech community, in a single nation, in one century.[32]

That is not to say, however, that the Niebuhrs' German language and lineage had not helped them in their theological education and early publications. Gustav had read and reviewed German church historian Adolf Harnack's work as early as 1902.[33] Both theologian brothers read Karl Barth, Emil Brunner, Dietrich Bonhoeffer, and Paul Tillich before they were available in English translation, and had a hand in bringing Bonhoeffer and Tillich to the United States.[34] Helmut had translated Tillich's *The Religious Situation* for English publication in 1926, and his adaptation of Ernst Troeltsch culminated in his own most enduring work, *Christ and Culture*.[35] Reinhold's bilingual facility helped in his various European tours and reportage after both world wars. Walter's

31. Schmidt, "Rhetoric of Survival," 2:207.
32. Heinz Kloss, cited in Eichoff, "German Language in America," 1:230.
33. Chrystal, *Father's Mantle*, 71.
34. Fox, *Reinhold Niebuhr*, 188.
35. Diefenthaler, *H. Richard Niebuhr*, 21.

Life Need Never Be Sad or Lonely

bilingualism enabled him to work effectively as a war correspondent, playwright, and filmmaker between 1915 and 1930. Hulda translated and introduced, along with Ursula's sister, Barbara Keppel-Compton, a work of German developmental psychology, Fritz Kunkel's *What It Means to Grow Up*.[36]

With family resettlement accomplished and questions of language and lineage behind them, the children of Lydia Hosto Niebuhr began to make names for themselves. Hulda published a collection of children's stories, *Greatness Passing By*, in 1931. The following year, Reinhold's first book of social ethics, *Moral Man and Immoral Society*, was published, and his first and only public exchange with brother H. Richard appeared in *The Christian Century*.[37] The thirties also brought the rise and fall of Walter's Beacon Films corporation, and a succession of jobs producing motion pictures for the Tennessee Valley Authority, Civilian Conservation Corps, and the Sloan Foundation. Reinhold followed in "Big Brother Sylvest's" political tracks, running unsuccessfully on the Socialist Party ticket for seats in the New York State Senate and the Unites States Congress. His disappointment with these defeats are mirrored in his rather pessimistic and apocalyptic *Reflections on the End of an Era* in 1934. During the following year, each of the theologian siblings published: Hulda, *Ventures in Dramatics*; H. Richard, coauthored with Wilhelm Pauck and William Miller, *The Church against the World*; and Reinhold, *An Interpretation of Christian Ethics*. In 1937, H. Richard published his theological rethinking of his more sociological first book, *The Kingdom of God in America*, and Reinhold published his first collection of sermonic essays, *Beyond Tragedy*. In 1939 Reinhold presented the prestigious Gifford Lectures at New College, University of Edinburgh, Scotland, later to be published as *The Nature and Destiny of Man*, generally regarded as his magnum opus.

Meanwhile, Walter observed his fiftieth birthday in the hospital where he was receiving treatment for depression and a

---

36. Caldwell, *Mysterious Mantle*, 60.

37. H. Richard Niebuhr, "Grace of Doing Nothing"; Reinhold Niebuhr, "Must We Do Nothing?"; H. Richard Niebuhr, "Communication."

growing problem with alcoholism. The 1930s brought his troubled career and business ventures to the depths of the economic depression that engulfed much of the Western world. He and his family moved about the country from job to job even more frequently than his maternal grandfather had half a century earlier, but without Hosto's success. Walter's easy and gregarious way with other people and his early athletic prowess and charm helped him as a fraternity man in college. He was a gifted writer, and though deaf since his tour of army duty with Pershing in Mexico, wrote and directed films and plays in Europe, and produced a number of educational and propaganda movies in the states. But a series of unwise business decisions, unscrupulous partners, and the advent of sound movies drove him to a serious drinking problem. He was admitted to a rehabilitation program for alcoholics in 1940. Brother Reinhold was paying Walter's bills, including the tuition for niece Carol's schooling.[38]

Reinhold, on the other hand, was at the height of his intellectual powers. In addition to the two-volume publication of the Gifford Lectures, the 1940s brought out his *Christianity and Power Politics* and *The Children of Light and the Children of Darkness*, among others. Along with Union colleague John Bennett, he founded *Christianity and Crisis*, a journal advocating US involvement in the war and challenging the easy isolationist pacifism of many church leaders.[39] His political star arose and stayed aloft during and after the war. In 1948 he served as a consultant in the Truman State Department and appeared on the cover of *TIME* magazine's silver anniversary issue.[40] While Hulda was working on her Kunkel translation, H. Richard published *The Meaning of Revelation*.

In early 1946, the Niebuhr mother-daughter team moved from Riverside Drive in New York to Chalmers Place in Chicago. Hulda accepted a call to teach at the Presbyterian College of Christian Education, adjacent to and affiliated with McCormick

---

38. Fox, *Reinhold Niebuhr*, 206, 211, 228.
39. Fox, *Reinhold Niebuhr*, 196–97.
40. Reinhold Niebuhr, "Faith for Lenten Age."

Life Need Never Be Sad or Lonely

Theological Seminary. Mütterchen, now age seventy-five, followed her daughter and housemate back to the Midwest. Nearly two decades in New York, surrounded by her children and grandchildren and the teenage girls of her classes, marked only a stop along the way. There was to be no retirement from her vocation. She would have another go at the role of the seminary professor's mother. With Reinhold at Union, the role seemed like exile. With Hulda at McCormick, it was a homecoming of sorts. "Now Mother has a new congregation," Hulda laughed. "A lot of the faculty children and young people come by our house and Mother is always planning something for them or helping them in some way."[41]

Lydia Niebuhr became a prominent and important member of the seminary community and neighborhood in which Hulda worked, first as an associate professor in the college and, in 1952, as a full professor and the first woman in the seminary faculty. Mütterchen was known as "McCormick's unofficial first lady" and the "fairy godmother of Chalmers Place."[42] Hulda wrote, "Mother has been very active on Chalmers Place, our faculty row. When she sits on the porch . . . there are always faculty and student and other neighborhood children about. When there is no school or they are for some reason looking for something to engage their interest, they come asking, 'What can we do today?'"[43] Her "week-day activities" from the Detroit and New York parish years, fostering a social spirit and putting Christian principles into practice, found another new home. Though her own grandchildren were more than a thousand miles away, Mütterchen delighted in sharing her "healthful, life-building . . . channels for self-expression" with the children of her Chicago neighborhood.[44]

Helen Haroutunian, a McCormick faculty spouse, reflected on the Niebuhr women with Elizabeth Caldwell, describing them as a creative team at work with the community's children: "It got so that it would be all the children in the neighborhood, whether

41. Hulda Niebuhr, "Letter to Theodore Braun" (Jan. 31, 1959), para. 4.
42. *Chicago Daily News*, "Mrs. Niebuhr's Day," para. 1.
43. Hulda Niebuhr, "Letter to Theodore Braun" (Jan. 31, 1959), para. 4.
44. Caldwell, *Mysterious Mantle*, 104.

they were seminary children or not, were included. And Hulda and her mother got to know all these people. And it wasn't one of these steamrolling, aggressive things. It was just patience and time. It was an outlet for her mother's creativity, and, I think, for Hulda's, too."[45]

Lydia initiated and organized two annual neighborhood parades, a spring Memorial Day event known as "Everything on Wheels" and a "Lighthouse Parade" in the early autumn. These traditions survived in the Chalmers Place neighborhood long after McCormick Seminary relocated to the Hyde Park area of Chicago's far South Side in the 1970s. Lydia had been fond of parades for years. Photos from Lincoln and Detroit show historical precedents for the Chicago wheel parade, with Sunday school "rally day" and summer Independence Day events featuring the children and their bicycles, tricycles, scooters, wagons, and baby carriages adorned with brightly colored decorations and flags. For the McCormick community, these seasonal activities brought a festive opening and closing to the academic year that included the smallest of children and integrated the seminary and its neighborhood with a cooperative spirit. That is, it became another of Mother Niebuhr's congregations, as Hulda had said.[46]

The year 1946 signaled this delightful new beginning for Mütterchen and her charismatic ministry with other people's children. But it was also a year of great family sadness, when her own eldest son died. Walter's health and career had deteriorated since his return from Europe in 1930, though it seems that his "enabling" siblings protected their mother from many of the more unpleasant details. Especially since his hospitalization for alcoholism in 1941, Walter worked only sporadically. From 1941 until 1944, he was chief librarian of the Astoria, New York, studios of the US Army Signal Corps. He was president of HVN Film Associates, New York City, at the time of his sudden death from a heart attack in

45. Helen Haroutunian, interview with Elizabeth Caldwell, Apr. 1, 1987.

46. Marshall Scott, interview with author, May 17, 1989. Scott became president of McCormick Seminary in 1952, finding Hulda Niebuhr an already well-established "liberal leader of the faculty."

Life Need Never Be Sad or Lonely

September 1946. A biographer has yet to sort through the details of Walter Niebuhr's many jobs, business ventures, and art. At the time of Walter's funeral in New York, Reinhold was in Germany and wrote this assessment to Ursula:

> I had a whole batch of letters from you, all about Walter's death. . . . I am sorry to be away through all these trials. Had letters from Hulda and Helmut today. I think the funeral helped Beulah. She chose the "Lead Kindly Light" hymn because Walter hummed it so much. Her willingness to forget all the suffering Walter caused and remember only his faithfulness to her is quite touching.[47]

When Reinhold returned to New York, he wrote his grieving sister-in-law, Beulah, a letter of sympathy in which he paid tribute to his late brother and encouraged her to embrace any "secret sense of relief" that might mingle with her sorrow:

> Actually you have a perfect right to such a sense. Walter was not likely to improve greatly in mental or physical health and might have become an almost impossible burden to those who loved him. It was well that he could go while you can still have pleasant memories of his loyalty. We can leave him safely to the Father of mercies who will know how to complete our own sorry and incomplete lives.[48]

In 1947, Elmhurst College granted an honorary doctorate of literature to Hulda Niebuhr. When she had been of college age as a young woman in Lincoln, Illinois, Elmhurst was a pre-seminary for boys (as young as fourteen) who would either further their education at Eden Seminary or accept a position in an Evangelical Synod parish as a church musician or parochial schoolteacher. Her mother had called for a comparable women's school, the Oakwood Institute in Cincinnati, and brother Helmut had led Elmhurst toward coeducation in the twenties, after which it developed a reputation as a church-related teachers' college. But Hulda had had to reach

---

47. Reinhold Niebuhr to Ursula Niebuhr, Sept. 10, 1946, in U. Niebuhr, *Remembering Reinhold Niebuhr*, 203–4.
48. Reinhold Niebuhr, "Letter to Beulah Niebuhr" (1946), para. 4.

beyond the Evangelical Synod to Boston and Columbia Universities, and between 1918 and 1928, she attracted other Evangelical women to Boston just as her theologian brothers had drawn their peers to Yale. During a time when only men served on the national board of Evangelical Sunday schools as officers and departmental and committee chairs, Hulda Niebuhr was superintendent of the children's division. When she went to work for the Presbyterians in New York, her reputation as a leader in religious education only grew within her own denomination. When she came to Chicago, Elmhurst College seized the opportunity to honor her pioneering ministry and add luster to its diamond jubilee commencement. Though the Oakwood Institute had not survived the Great Depression, Lydia must have found some satisfaction in the fact that Elmhurst, now coed, had honored her daughter with a doctorate.[49]

In 1953 the honorary tables were turned. Lindenwood College of St. Charles, Missouri, presented Lydia with an honorary doctorate. Hulda accompanied her mother in this triumphant homecoming to the community where Gustav Niebuhr had served the Evangelical Synod and Emmaus Homes half a century earlier. Lindenwood was a small, women's liberal arts college affiliated with the Presbyterian Church. At the Founders' Day convocation during which Lydia received the degree, Hulda gave the address. "Spiritual Progenitors" was a thinly veiled tribute to Mütterchen that celebrated the personal, interactive, and caring role of the faithful religious educator. The doctoral citation read:

> For loving dedication of intelligence and imagination to home, church and school; for continuing exercise of mind and spirit in stimulation of those around her; for that conspicuous enrichment of human letters and human life which is her children's amplification of her devotion and wisdom: the degree of Doctor of Humanities.[50]

---

49. Duckert, "Interpreters of Our Faith." See also the file on Hulda Niebuhr in the Eden Theological Seminary archives, Saint Louis.

50. *Lindenwood College Bulletin*, "Mrs. Lydia Niebuhr," 3.

Life Need Never Be Sad or Lonely

The Christian Century noticed the honor in a front-page unsigned editorial, in November 1953, entitled "Honor Where Honor Is Due":

> Honorary Degrees are one of the subjects we usually regard as in the province of Simeon Stylites. But did you happen to notice the news item about the Doctor of Humanities degree conferred the other day by Lindenwood College . . . ? The recipient was a tiny, 83-year-old, bright-eyed woman who undoubtedly was the most surprised person there. . . . If anyone asked her what her career had been she would have said, "parsonage wife and mother." But out of the parsonages which Lydia shared with the Rev. Gustav Niebuhr there came the three children . . . who have made such a mark on the life of the churches, as well as a body of pastoral labors which organized new congregations, revived dormant ones, established philanthropic institutions and injected vigor into the church press.

Lydia's old Bethel friend, Detroit journalist John Finlayson, also noticed Dr. Niebuhr's honor and hoped to write about it too. In her February 1954, response of futile protest at this possibility, she armed Finlayson with details to correct the record and draw herself back from center stage:

> It was very gracious of you to take note of the Lindenwood event. If and when you write a story, I trust the *St. Louis Post-Dispatch* report will be amended to contain a reference to my husband's ministry in Lincoln, Ill., as pastor of St. John's Evangelical Church. We lived there from 1902 to 1915 and it is there the children grew up.[51]

She did not sign this or any known letter as "Dr. Niebuhr" but simply "Lydia Niebuhr." She often returned in her thoughts to Lincoln, and in 1952, returned in person to help the Deaconess Hospital celebrate its fiftieth anniversary. She had helped the planning committee prepare its history of the hospital and deaconess society, especially translating the earliest records from German.[52]

51. L. Niebuhr, "Letter to John Finlayson."
52. Gimbel, "Few Notes."

Lydia Hosto Niebuhr

The anniversary program listed among "Our Guests of Honor" "Mrs. Gustave [sic] Niebuhr, earliest former trustee present (1903–1915) and wife of the late Rev. G. Niebuhr, administrator of Deaconess Hospital 1902–1913."[53] Lydia's sister, Adele Hosto, had returned to Lincoln to live after retiring from her long ministry in Chicago as a parish deaconess. She and many admiring friends made Lincoln a pleasant visit and homecoming, as well as a place of fond memories.

In April 1959, a brief month after Hulda's seventieth birthday and before her anticipated retirement from McCormick, the eldest of Mother Niebuhr's children died. Like her brother Walter and Hosto grandparents, her death came suddenly in heart failure. Helen Haroutunian recalled to Elizabeth Caldwell, "I remember it was kind of sudden. [Hulda] had heart problems, and no one knew, and before she could retire, she died. She was sick a very short time and it was quite a surprise and a shock, and we thought it would kill her mother and wondered what she would do."[54]

The Niebuhrs' Chalmers Place housekeeper, Ella Mae Smith, spoke with simple and perceptive wisdom in her recollection to Hulda's biographer that "Hulda didn't want to retire and so she just died." Whether true or not for daughter, Mother Niebuhr was once again faced with the threat of homelessness. "Mrs. Niebuhr was the backbone of the house," Smith also recalled.[55] But without her daughter the provider, Mütterchen was indeed homeless; and just as she had had to make reluctant moves from Lincoln after Gustav's death, from Detroit after Reinhold's resignation from Bethel, and from his New York household when he married, so now Mother Niebuhr's career as an itinerant parsonage daughter, wife, and mother continued. In her ninetieth year, Lydia Hosto Niebuhr had already lived in at least fifteen different homes in five states and with four different configurations of family members. She had already said sad farewells to parents, husband, and three of her five offspring. But her long pilgrimage was not yet complete.

53. St. John's Evangelical Church, "Service of Thanksgiving," 3.
54. Helen Haroutunian, interview with Elizabeth Caldwell, Apr. 1, 1987.
55. Smith, "Interview with Elizabeth Caldwell."

Life Need Never Be Sad or Lonely

Fortunately, she thrived on an inner strength, a childlike trust and simple faith that impressed young and old. McCormick friend Helen Haroutunian remembered to Elizabeth Caldwell both Niebuhr women and stressed that their identities as part of the seminary and neighborhood communities were inseparable. "I had the greatest deal of respect for both of them and began thinking how marvelous old Mrs. Niebuhr was. She was a widow, and she had no love of her own, in a sense. But she had a tremendous life, and it came from the inside." Haroutunian also recalled the gift of a book from the Niebuhrs, a collection of letters from the court of the eighteenth-century Pietist Nikolas von Zinzendorf. She wasn't sure if the gift was the idea of a mother or daughter or both, but she believed the point of the book and its letters was to promote a simple faith as trust. "The hard things you suffer are God's way of turning your attention to Him so that you should be grateful for this trial. This is cleansing you. This is teaching you what you need to know."[56]

Mütterchen bore her misfortune with such pietistic assurance of faith, and in much the same way that an old woman at Bethel had in 1928, prompting these admiring reflections from her pastor son:

> The way Mrs.— bears her pains and awaits her ultimate and certain dissolution with childlike faith and inner serenity is an achievement which philosophers might well envy. . . . There is a quality in the lives of unschooled people, if they have made good use of the school of life and pain, which wins my admiration much more than anything you can find in effete circles. There is less of that whining rebellion against life's misfortunes, less morbid introspection and more faith in the goodness of God. And that faith is, whatever the cynics may say, really ultimate wisdom. Mrs.— has had a hard life, raised a large family under great difficulties, is revered by her children, respected by her friends, and she has learned to

---

56. Helen Haroutunian, interview with Elizabeth Caldwell, Apr. 1, 1987.

view the difficult future with quiet courage as she surveys the painful and yet happy past with sincere gratitude.[57]

Alone now in Chicago, Lydia mourned the loss of her dear daughter but did not grieve over her own misfortune in being displaced once again. Without Hulda, and with Reinhold's lingering paralysis and disability, it now fell to Helmut to care for their mother. After the funeral in Chicago, she would join him and Florence in Connecticut.[58]

---

57. Reinhold Niebuhr, *Leaves from the Notebook*, 189–90.
58. H. Richard Niebuhr, "Letter to Carol Niebuhr Buchanan" (1959).

5

Happiness Is in Our Hands

Lydia with her sister, Adele Hosto, for Lydia's ninetieth birthday in 1959.

Lydia Hosto Niebuhr

THE CHICAGO DAILY NEWS took note of the coming 1959 Memorial Day weekend activities in the neighborhood around Chalmers Place. "It'll Be Mrs. Niebuhr's Day," when the McCormick community will celebrate the Memorial Day "Wheel Parade" one last time with its creator, the newspaper announced. "Her Children Will Parade," read the subheading. "Saturday will belong to Mrs. Lydia Niebuhr," said the article.[1] The accompanying photograph showed "the fairy godmother of Chalmers Place" discussing the upcoming "annual spring festival for the children" with seven smiling youngsters, "her 'other family.'" Despite the anticipated fun on Saturday, "McCormick's unofficial first lady" was sad to be moving away from Chicago in June, "to the east, where she will divide her time with her famous sons."[2]

After the burial of her firstborn, Hulda, near her husband's grave in Lincoln, Illinois, Lydia moved to Connecticut. There she joined the household of her youngest, Helmut Richard, and his wife Florence. From their Hamden home she frequently visited Reinhold in New York, by then nearing retirement from Union Seminary. Reinhold's son Christopher remembers unfortunate incidents in the kitchen of his aunt Florence and uncle Helmut, when Mütterchen would warm milk on the stove for a bedtime drink and forget to turn off the gas burner.[3] Relations between Lydia and Florence were only slightly less strained than those with Ursula. Summer vacations as an extended family were one thing; constant living under one roof was something else again. By year's end, Lydia had agreed to return to Lincoln where she could spend her last days with her sister, Adele Hosto.[4]

After forty-five years, Lydia and her youngest surviving sibling were reunited in the Illinois town where Lydia had overseen the deaconess society and hospital affairs and Adele had been consecrated an Evangelical deaconess. Lydia introduced some of her hobbies to the other residents of the nursing home, in its first years

1. *Chicago Daily News*, "Mrs. Niebuhr's Day," para. 3.
2. *Chicago Daily News*, "Mrs. Niebuhr's Day," para. 3.
3. C. Niebuhr, "Letter," para. 3.
4. Carol Niebuhr Buchanan, interview with author, Mar. 17, 1993.

Happiness Is in Our Hands

of operation as a residence for retired deaconesses like Sister Adele Hosto. "Blue printing" and the construction of miniature stained glass windows and lanterns were among the handwork projects Lydia brought back to her old hometown. Marguerite Eisen wrote of the crafts and their effect on visitors to her friend's former home in Chicago.

> The children on the McCormick campus love to visit Mrs. Niebuhr's home not just to see her hobbies, which fascinate them but to visit with their kind friend who loves them. In a recent letter Mrs. Niebuhr tells of helping some young friends achieve stained glass compositions of their own. "It was worth all the effort for more delighted youngsters you could not find."
>
> Visiting Mrs. Niebuhr's home is a delightful experience and as one admires the charming handmade creative arts one realizes how valuable is the wise use of time and talents and that not only beauty, but happiness is in our hands![5]

Lydia kept her hands busy and happy, creating small objects of beauty to give away. Because of her stained glass work, she received a new soldering gun for her eighty-fifth birthday. At eighty-two she planted two hundred tulip bulbs. She continued to enjoy photography and her collections of ferns and seashells, and her embroidery, cross-stitching, hooked-rag rugs and applique designs remained constant companions. She sewed all of her own clothing, coats, and hats, and at eighty-six made a new winter overcoat and a velvet dress. She played chess with grandson Richard by mail. She played the piano as she had for her father's churches as a youngster. When she was eighty-nine, she made gifts, wrapped, and mailed them for all of her grandchildren and great grandchildren. For her ninetieth Christmas birthday, her friends sent her ninety white roses, and a cash gift was sent to Albert Schweitzer's clinic in her honor. For her ninety-first birthday, Lydia took the train from Lincoln to Chicago for a visit with a young couple at McCormick.

5. Eisen, "Letter," 3.

Lydia Hosto Niebuhr

When she returned, she and her sister hosted a New Year's tea for fourteen guests, with table decorations that her great-grandchildren had made and sent her for Christmas.[6] Her thank-you note to granddaughter Carol Buchanan and her family, dated January 2, 1961, may have been her last correspondence.[7]

Lydia and Sister Adele enjoyed one another's company for one year in Lincoln. Old and new Lincoln friends also enjoyed the company of a nearly legendary former St. John parsonage wife. "Lydia Niebuhr was an elegant lady in her own right," wrote Ray Gimbel, admiring St. John parishioner and local historian. "It was always a lift to visit with her, she was as gracious as queen."[8] When she had left the East in December 1959, Reinhold wrote to June Bingham, then preparing his biography, *Courage to Change*: "Yesterday I went to the station to bid my mother a sad farewell. She will be ninety on Christmas day and I doubt whether I will ever see her again. Such are the sadnesses of old age."[9] Little more than a year later, Reinhold's doubt was confirmed. Dr. Lydia Mathilde Hosto Niebuhr died on January 24, 1961, in Lincoln, at ninety-one. In Reinhold's words, she died "without suffering, after only two hours of illness."[10]

According to Helmut, who had become responsible for his mother's affairs since Reinhold's stroke, "she went out like a light at a little before seven o'clock in the morning."[11] In a February letter to niece Carol, Helmut described the circumstances of the Friday funeral for beloved Mütterchen:

> We buried her on a bitter cold day. But relatives from St. Louis and friends from McCormick Seminary were there as well as many Lincoln friends. It is the way she wanted to go for she dreaded a long illness and we must be content. It will take some time before we get used to the idea

6. Gimbel, "Few Notes."
7. L. Niebuhr, "Letter to Carol Niebuhr Buchanan."
8. Gimbel, "Letter," para. 5.
9. Reinhold Niebuhr, "Letter to June Bingham," para. 2.
10. Fox, *Reinhold Niebuhr*, 270.
11. H. Richard Niebuhr, "Letter to Carol Niebuhr Buchanan" (1961).

of her not being in this world but she was fully active in it to the end and there is much to be grateful for.[12]

Neither Carol, her mother, Walter's widow Beulah, nor Uncle Reinhold were able to attend services for Mütterchen. Reinhold, pecking on his typewriter with his one good hand, wrote to Beulah: "Thank you so much for your letter of sympathy about mother's death. You are right: we were very close and my marriage was a difficult chapter in her life. But she adjusted herself to all things with grace and infinite capacity for trying new responsibilities."[13]

McCormick had its own memorial service in Chicago as well. The words and images of Ted Campbell's eulogy there echo those of Paul Lehmann, quoted in the introduction of this biography:

> Jesus said to his disciples: "suffer the little children to come unto me . . . for of such is the kingdom of heaven." Surely, then, Lydia Niebuhr had more contact with the kingdom of heaven than anyone else I know. For ninety-one years she kept young in her faith by what she learned from the children to whom the kingdom belongs. And her example, her life, has reached us all.[14]

Ursula Niebuhr later offered a different reading of the same data and metaphor in reaction to the author's thesis:

> Mrs. Lydia Niebuhr was so protected by her wonderful children that she became as a sheltered child of the family from whom unpleasant facts and complications were not to be discussed or known. Perhaps this was not fair to her, yet this was the pattern and many remarked that her gifts for dealing with children seemed to make her more and more childlike.[15]

Whether childlike or childish, Mütterchen's love for children and their love for her remained to the end. When she was sixty years old, she went to Europe with her family. This was to be Lydia's only

12. H. Richard Niebuhr, "Letter to Carol Niebuhr Buchanan" (1961).
13. Reinhold Niebuhr, "Letter to Beulah Niebuhr" (1961).
14. Campbell, "Lydia Niebuhr," 1.
15. U. Niebuhr, "Letter," 2.

visit to her immigrant parents' homeland. Helmut was on sabbatical there. Walter and Beulah were preparing to return from their decade there. Reinhold paid a brief visit to England in order to be introduced to Ursula's family before their marriage. Hulda had interest in meeting some of her German cousins. The only extant correspondence from Mother Niebuhr during this European visit is a postcard to Eleanore Merckel, an early adolescent girl from Bethel Church. With childlike enthusiasm, Lydia reported that she was having a "great time in Germany, Belgium and Holland." The card, postmarked September 8, 1930, pictured two Dutch teenage girls with a younger brother between them. Lydia's message connected her love for children in general, her love for Eleanore, and her enthusiasm to share photos of her experience when she next returned to Detroit. "This coming week I go on to Austria and Italy," she wrote. "Yesterday I went out to a little fishing village to take pictures of Dutch children in their native costumes. I hope you will enjoy them when I bring them to Detroit."[16]

Sister Adele saw to it that Mütterchen's granddaughter Carol received a legacy of her late grandmother's handwork. The shipment included pieced patchwork quilts, rag rugs that had covered floors in Chicago and Lincoln, embroidered pillowcases, crocheted tablecloths, and collections of shells and ferns, all to be added to Carol's existing inventory of Mütterchen's eight-millimeter movies and still photos, stained glass creations, wardrobe of doll clothing, and commemorative anniversary silverware already on hand. Checking to see that these family treasures arrived safely, Adele wrote in October 1961:

> I miss Mütterchen so much, life doesn't seem the same without her, but she was real weak and frail this past year especially, and many evenings she would say she couldn't take another step. But she kept doing things and had much joy out of working with shells with a group of smaller boys and girls from our church. I was so happy to have her with me this past year.[17]

16. L. Niebuhr, "Postcard to Eleanore Merckel."
17. A. Hosto, "Letter."

Mütterchen's love for children also was written into her last will and testament. Five of ten shares of her estate were to be divided among her two surviving sons and Walter's widow, Beulah. The other five were to be distributed among McCormick Theological Seminary, the interracial work of the United Presbyterian Church, the Board of Pensions and Relief of the Evangelical and Reformed Church, and the Department of Church World Service of the National Council of Churches "for overseas relief, especially of children."[18]

When Ralph Abele was preparing his 1959 essay, "A Woman Named Lydia," he had to rely on Hulda for biographical help. Mother Niebuhr was reluctant to talk about herself in any way. Theodore Braun, like Abele a former Niebuhr colleague at Bethel Church, was the editor of the *United Church Herald* in 1959. In response to Braun's intervention, requesting more information to assist Abele with his essay, Hulda explained to the editor that there were certain constraints with which she and any biographer would have to labor: "Mother hopes you will not any time quote her, and I send you this on condition that I am not quoted."[19]

This biographer has been frustrated in learning that these constraints persist, more than sixty years later. Much personal and family correspondence was evidently destroyed by Helmut at the time of Hulda's death. Though Lydia Niebuhr is known from Evangelical Synod records to have presented at least four addresses before large synod audiences between 1919 and 1928, the monthly *Bethel Bulletin* (replaced in 1921 by the weekly Bethel Church bulletin), for which she was the anonymous editor, made no such references.[20] The church newsletter did, however, refer to every other family member's activities, including Walter's and Helmut's

18. H. Richard Niebuhr, "Letter to Carol Niebuhr Buchanan" (1961).

19. Hulda Niebuhr, "Letter to Theodore Braun" (Feb. 3, 1959), 2.

20. *Evangelical Herald*, "Women's Page," notes that Lydia led several sessions for the Missionary Education Committee of the Evangelical Synod Women's Union in a discussion of the book *A Straight Way toward Tomorrow*. The Bethel Church bulletin does indicate that Lydia addressed the annual Michigan convention of Evangelical Young People's and Sunday School workers; but no manuscript has been found ("Notes" [June 17, 1928] 3).

weddings and Sister Adele's frequent visits to Detroit. Her insistence on anonymity throughout her long life and her sensitivity to children and others are a part of her legacy, and these characteristics must qualify the Louis Goebel metaphor, crowning Lydia Hosto Niebuhr as "the Queen Bee of American Theologians."

But, despite her wish for invisibility, her lifetime of service has left a trail to be traced and remembered. That trail is part of the historical record that carries lessons about change, the role of church in society, the value of spiritual formation, the variety of models for ministry, and the role of women in this culture. Because of the remarkable contribution of her children, we may bring other questions to the life of this particular mother, seeking to locate the source of their genius. To what extent, for example, did her ever-youthful faith, "kept young . . . by what she learned from the children to whom the kingdom belongs,"[21] shape the vocations of Hulda, Walter, Reinhold, and H. Richard Niebuhr? Can we link her "infinite capacity for trying new responsibilities"[22] to the pioneering missionary work of her father or the picaresque career of her artist son, Walter?

Lydia Hosto Niebuhr spent her life much as her deaconess sister Adele had, "administering the charities of the church" and expressing the irenic Evangelical faith in practical deeds of loving service.[23] Despite their subordinate status as women, the Evangelical deaconesses were activists in and beyond the parish. Lydia bridged the life of the single professional deaconess with that of the traditional "parsonage wife and mother." Though she took no formal pledge, as Sister Adele had, to be obedient, willing, and faithful to apply the love of Christ in the Evangelical parish, Lydia nonetheless exercised the deaconess virtues. She served within public spheres where the boundaries between family and parish, motherhood and ministry, remained unclear. Her vocation transcended the various roles of pastoral assistant; organist; choir director; youth leader; Sunday school teacher, supervisor, and

---

21. Braun, "In Memoriam."
22. Reinhold Niebuhr, "Letter to Beulah Niebuhr" (1961).
23. Gimbel, *Story of St. John*, 34.

superintendent; missions promoter; and activities coordinator. Though a woman of her age, yet she was a pioneering missionary and spiritual progenitor for future women in church vocations. Though bound, she was free. Though apparently restricted by the idealized images of the "dutiful daughter," "faithful wife," "perpetual child," and "wise old woman" (as psychotherapist Madeline Harris has described them), yet she may not be accused of living her life "on a pedestal."[24] Though subordinate as a servant who wished always to remain unquoted and invisible, she was a reigning matriarch whose social reach was extensive and whose public influence was considerable. Though "busy with something external" and social for a lifetime,[25] her inner life remains shrouded in a mysteriously impenetrable privacy.

As a theological helpmate to father, husband, son, and daughter, Lydia Hosto Niebuhr exhibited a strength of character that enabled her, in her own words, "to live the Christian life under all circumstances,"[26] and in son Reinhold's, to adjust "herself to all things with grace and infinite capacity for trying new responsibilities."[27] As a de facto parish deaconess in a variety of settings in two denominations, she extended and promoted the "spiritual welfare of the church among its members,"[28] accomplishing the "upright serving of social love" for which the deaconess movement leaders had once prayed.[29] The eulogy of Rabbi Abraham Heschel for Reinhold apply equally to his mother: "Niebuhr's life was a song in the form of deeds, a song that will go on forever."[30]

A tall stone cross marked "Niebuhr" casts its shadow across the four graves of Lydia, Gustav, Hulda, and Sister Adele Hosto. Only a few people at St. John United Church of Christ in Lincoln, Illinois, know who the Hostos and Niebuhrs were or what their

24. Harris, *Down from the Pedestal*.
25. H. Richard Niebuhr, "Letter to Reinhold Niebuhr," para. 3.
26. L. Niebuhr, "Week-Day Activities."
27. Reinhold Niebuhr, "Letter to Beulah Niebuhr" (1961).
28. Gimbel et al., *Story of St. John*, 35.
29. Gimbel et al., *Story of St. John*, 21.
30. Heschel, "Last Farewell," 63.

family's legacies might represent. A few more may know that the nearby Abraham Lincoln Memorial Hospital once had a connection, other than proximity, to the church. But the deaconess society and their sponsoring Evangelical Synod are mostly forgotten, along with the irenic and pietistic spirit that drove them to found hospitals and maintain deaconess houses as "servants of the Lord Jesus, servants of the sick and poor for Jesus' sake, and servants to each other."[31] Yet there is a living legacy in the continuing scholarly debate over the Niebuhrs as a significant twentieth-century family. May this biography of the matriarch serve to ground the debate in the history of the Niebuhrs' and Hostos' spiritual home, the deaconess movement within the German Evangelical Synod of North America. Alongside the prophetic "father's mantle" of Gustav and the "mysterious mantle" that was Hulda's, we lay the patchwork quilt of Lydia Hosto Niebuhr, pieced together out of many lives.

---

31. Chrystal, *Father's Mantle*, 69.

A Bibliographical Essay

LIKE THE PERSON, THE sources for the life of Lydia Hosto Niebuhr are hidden behind other family members. The biography of Lydia Hosto Niebuhr began in 1987 as a graduate student's history class research paper. Professors Rosemary Skinner Keller and Josef Barton inspired and encouraged the pursuit of this researcher's challenge. A student colleague, Elizabeth Caldwell, was approaching her decision to write the biography of Hulda Niebuhr for her dissertation, and we began a fruitful collaboration that included several joint presentations on the Niebuhr mother-daughter team. Caldwell's work was published as *Mysterious Mantle: The Biography of Hulda Niebuhr* (1992). The lives of Mother Niebuhr and her daughter were mysteriously intertwined, and this writer found himself intrigued by the possibility of presenting the nearly invisible woman in the background as the principal subject of a biography. Caldwell uncovered mutually useful primary sources in the archives of McCormick Theological Seminary, Chicago; Madison Avenue Presbyterian Church, New York; and Immanuel Bethel United Church of Christ, Royal Oak (Detroit), Michigan. Her oral interviews with McCormick colleagues of the Niebuhr women were also most helpful.

The trail of sources then led back to a seminary colleague's work, broadening the scope of research to other Niebuhr family members. William G. Chrystal collected, organized, and analyzed Niebuhr materials while a student at Eden Theological Seminary

A Bibliographical Essay

in St. Louis. Chrystal worked in the Evangelical Synod of North America archives there, and as a result published several articles and books on the Niebuhrs and their formative influences. His fellow seminarians were awed that a classmate could have published, before graduation, *Young Reinhold Niebuhr: His Early Writings* (1977). Chrystal later published *A Father's Mantle: The Legacy of Gustav Niebuhr* (1982), and in so doing amassed his own impressive archive of Niebuhriana. Chrystal has done the most of any Niebuhr scholar to take seriously the unique theological heritage of the Evangelical Synod.

The major biographies of Reinhold Niebuhr are important secondary sources as well. The place to begin is June Bingham, *Courage to Change: An Introduction to the Life and Thought of Reinhold Niebuhr* (first published in 1961 and reissued in 1992). Richard Fox's *Reinhold Niebuhr: A Biography* (1985) is a treasury of research and an artful blend of intellectual and social history, but its interpretive framework is seriously flawed. Ronald Stone has two important biographical contributions, *Prophet to Politicians* (1972) and *Professor Reinhold Niebuhr: Mentor to the Twentieth Century* (1992), the second of which gives proper credit to Niebuhr family influences. Charles Brown's intellectual biography, *Niebuhr and His Age* (1992), and Stone's second book are to be read as correctives to Richard Fox. The Niebuhr papers in the Manuscript Division of the Library of Congress, Washington, DC, are the largest single collection of primary sources, a sampling of which is to be found in Ursula Niebuhr, *Remembering Reinhold Niebuhr: Letters of Reinhold and Ursula M. Niebuhr* (1991).

Niebuhr family members have offered memories and insights. Carol Lydia Niebuhr Buchanan, daughter of Walter and Beulah Niebuhr, opened her home and family archive to this writer and William Chrystal, then preparing a biographical monograph on her father. This favored grandchild and heir to Mütterchen's gracious spirit provided more encouragement for the completion of this biography than any other single individual. Reinhold's widow, Ursula, and children, Christopher and Elisabeth; and H. Richard's son, Richard R., and grandson, R. Gustav, have patiently answered

A Bibliographical Essay

questions probing their family history. Sadly, the path to sources is full of cul-de-sacs, including H. Richard's destruction of family correspondence at the time of Hulda's death in 1959 (as reported by Richard Fox). An important discovery was the Hosto family. Ruth Weltge Rasche in St. Louis and Alfred Suhre and Anita Ullman in Alhambra, Illinois, helped with this dimension.

In addition to church records at St. John United Church of Christ, Lincoln, Illinois; Immanuel Bethel United Church of Christ, Royal Oak, Michigan; and Madison Avenue Presbyterian Church, New York City, New York, there were a few aged church members with valuable living memories of the Niebuhrs. The greatest untapped living sources were the Madison Avenue–New York (1930–45) teenagers and McCormick-Chicago (1946–59) children who sat in Lydia Niebuhr's classes or marched in her parades.

Bibliography

Abele, Ralph C. "A Woman Named Lydia." *United Church Herald* (Sept. 17, 1959) 10–12.
Ahlstrom, Sydney E. *A Religious History of the American People*. New Haven, CT: Yale University Press, 1972.
Baltzer, Herman. *Adolf Baltzer: The Story of Adolf Baltzer Taken in Part from His Association with the Evangelical Church of North America*. Translated by Caroline Baltzer. St. Louis: Eden, 1896.
Belleville News-Democrat. "Rev. W. H. Hosto Is Honored by Congregation." *Belleville News-Democrat* (Oct. 3, 1911).
Bethel Bulletin. Monthly newsletter, 1915–20. In Immanuel-Bethel United Church of Christ archives, Royal Oak, MI.
Bethel Church. *Bethel Year Book and Directory*. Annual report, multiple years. In Immanuel-Bethel United Church of Christ archives, Royal Oak, MI.
———. *Brief History of Bethel Church*. Twenty-fifth anniversary booklet, Oct. 1937. In Immanuel-Bethel United Church of Christ archives, Royal Oak, MI.
———. "A Farewell Tribute to Rev. Niebuhr and His Mother." Printed program, Oct. 1, 1928. In Immanuel-Bethel United Church of Christ archives, Royal Oak, MI.
———. *Retrospect and Prospect*. Year-end report, Dec. 1922. In Immanuel-Bethel United Church of Christ archives, Royal Oak, MI.
Bethel Church Council. "Minutes." Unpublished manuscript, typed. In Immanuel-Bethel United Church of Christ archives, Royal Oak, MI.
Bethel Church Frauenverein. "Minutes." Unpublished manuscript. In Immanuel-Bethel United Church of Christ archives, Royal Oak, MI.
Bingham, June. *Courage to Change: An Introduction to the Life and Thought of Reinhold Niebuhr*. New York: Scribner's Sons, 1961.
Board of Sunday Schools. *Sunday School Work in the Evangelical Synod of North America, 1916–1919: Official Report of the Second National Convention of*

Bibliography

Evangelical Sunday Schools. St Louis: Board of Sunday Schools, 1919. In Eden Theological Seminary archives, Saint Louis.

Bode, H. "Pastor Eduard Jakob Hosto, Feb. 14, 1833–Sept. 6, 1912." [In German.] *Friedensbote* 63 (Oct. 20, 1912) 662–63.

Braun, Theodore. "In Memoriam." *United Church Herald* (Aug. 1962) 7.

———. "Interview with Charles C. Brown." Audiotape, 1978. In the author's possession.

Brown, Dale W. *What Is Pietism?* Grand Rapids: Eerdmans, 1978.

Brown, Susan K. "Paradoxical Pastor." *St. Louis Post-Dispatch* (June 18, 1992).

Brueggemann, Walter A. *Ethos and Ecumenism, an Evangelical Blend: History of Eden Seminary, 1925–1975.* St. Louis: Eden, 1975.

———. *The Evangelical Catechism Revisited, 1847–1972.* St. Louis: Eden, 1972.

Bundy, Gloria. "Letter to John Clifford Helt." Mar. 26, 1993. In the author's possession.

Caldwell, Elizabeth. *A Mysterious Mantle: The Biography of Hulda Niebuhr.* Cleveland: Pilgrim, 1992.

Campbell, Ted. "Lydia Niebuhr." Eulogy, Jan. 1961. In McCormick Theological Seminary archives, Chicago.

Christian Century. "Honor Where Honor Is Due." *Christian Century* 70 (Nov. 11, 1953) 1.

Chrystal, William G. "'American' without Any 'If' and 'Buts': The Niebuhrs and the First World War." Unpublished manuscript, typed, n.d. In the author's possession.

———. "Father Saw the Path." In *Fellowship of Prayer: Lent 1987*, unnumbered pages. St. Louis: CBP, 1987.

———. *A Father's Mantle: The Legacy of Gustav Niebuhr.* New York: Pilgrim, 1982.

———. "Samuel D. Press: Teacher of the Niebuhrs." *Church History* 53 (Dec. 1984) 504–21.

Conzen, Kathleen Neils. "German-Americans and the Invention of Ethnicity." In *America and the Germans: An Assessment of a 300-Year History*, edited by Frank Trommler and Joseph McVeigh, 1:131–47. Philadelphia: University of Pennsylvania Press, 1985.

Crocco, Stephen. "President H. Richard Niebuhr: The Elmhurst Years." Unpublished manuscript, typed, Apr. 5, 1987. In the author's possession.

Denger, Florence. "Letter to Hulda Niebuhr." N.d. In Reinhold Niebuhr Papers, Library of Congress, Washington, DC.

Diefenthaler, Jon. *H. Richard Niebuhr: A Lifetime of Reflections on the Church and the World.* Macon: Mercer University Press, 1986.

Duckert, Mary. "Interpreters of Our Faith: Hulda Niebuhr." *A. D. Magazine* (Sept. 1976) 36–37.

Dunn, David, et al. *A History of the Evangelical and Reformed Church.* Philadelphia: Christian Education, 1961.

Eggleston, Margaret. *Womanhood in the Making.* New York: Doran, 1923.

Bibliography

Eichoff, Jürgen. "The German Language in America." In *America and the Germans: An Assessment of a 300-Year History*, edited by Frank Trommler and Joseph McVeigh, 1:223–40. Philadelphia: University of Pennsylvania Press, 1985.

Eisen, Marguerite. "Letter to John Clifford Helt." N.d., c. 1988. In the author's possession.

Evangelical Synod of North America. *Evangelical Catechism*. St. Louis: Eden, 1929.

Evangelical Herald. "The Women's Page." *Evangelical Herald* (Nov. 1, 1928) 874. In Eden Theological Seminary archives, Saint Louis.

Evangelische St. Johannes Gemeinde, Die. *Souvenir zum Goldenen Jubilaum der Evangelischen St. Johannes Gemeinde zu Lincoln, Illinois*. Pamphlet, Oct. 23, 1910.

Fowler, James W. *To See the Kingdom: The Theological Vision of H. Richard Niebuhr*. Nashville: Abingdon, 1974.

Fox, Richard. *Reinhold Niebuhr: A Biography*. New York: Pantheon, 1985.

Gimbel, Ray. "A Few Notes about Mrs. Niebuhr during the Period 1952 to 1961, Age 83–91." Handwritten manuscript, n.d. In St. John United Church of Christ archives, Lincoln, IL.

———. "Letter to John Clifford Helt." Jan. 6, 1986. In the author's possession.

Gimbel, Ray, et al. *The Story of St. John Church, Lincoln, Illinois, 1860–1960*. Lincoln, IL: St. John United Church of Christ, 1960.

Goebel, Louis. *Recollections*. Unpublished manuscript, typed and bound, 1959. In Eden Theological Seminary archives, Saint Louis.

Gunnemann, Louis. *A History of the United Church of Christ*. New York: Pilgrim, 1977.

Hansen, Marcus Lee. *The Immigrant in American History*. New York: Harper and Row, 1964.

Harris, Madeline. *Down from the Pedestal: Moving beyond Idealized Images of Womanhood*. New York: Doubleday, 1994.

Heilbrun, Carolyn G. *Writing a Woman's Life*. New York: Norton and Co., 1988.

Heschel, Abraham Joshua. "A Last Farewell." *Conservative Judaism* 25 (1971) 62–63.

Higham, John. *Strangers in the Land: Patterns of American Nativism, 1860–1925*. New Brunswick, NJ: Rutgers University Press, 1988.

Horstmann, Julius S., and Herbert H. Wernecke. *Through Four Centuries: The Story of the Beginnings of the Evangelical and Reformed Church, in the Old World and the New, from the Sixteenth to the Twentieth Century*. St. Louis: Eden, 1938.

Hosto, Adele. "Letter to Carol Niebuhr Buchanan." Oct. 29, 1961. Copy in the author's possession.

Hosto, Clara. "Letter to Elizabeth Weltge." May 12, 1901. Translated by Clara E. Weltge. In the author's possession.

Hurrle, John. "Letter to John Clifford Helt." Oct., 1993. In the author's possession.

Bibliography

Chicago Daily News. "It'll Be Mrs. Niebuhr's Day: Her Children Will Parade." *Chicago Daily News,* May 30, 1959.

Jerger, F. "Pastor Friederich August Wilhelm Weltge, October 5, 1852-September 4, 1928." [In German.] *Friedensbote* 79 (Oct. 7, 1928) 647.

Kamphausen, H. *The Story of the Religious Life in the Evangelical Synod of North America.* Translated by John W. Flucke. Cleveland: 1924.

Kimbrough, Mary. "Associate Pastor Role for Mother." *St. Louis Post-Dispatch,* Oct. 6, 1953.

Laaser, Robert O. *Our Beloved Eden: The Story of the Seminary.* St. Louis: Eden Theological Seminary Press, 1991.

Lehmann, Paul. "The Faith of Piety and the Piety of Faith." Audiotape of three unpublished lectures on the legacy of Reinhold Niebuhr, given at Eden Seminary, Webster Groves, MO, Apr. 1979.

Lincoln Daily News-Herald. "Rev. E.J. Hosto Died Suddenly Friday." *Lincoln Daily News-Herald,* Sept. 7, 1912.

Lindenwood College Bulletin. "Mrs. Lydia Niebuhr Receives Honorary Degree, Dr. Hulda Niebuhr Speaks, at Founders Day Convo." *Lindenwood College Bulletin* (Dec. 1953) 3–4.

McFaul, Thomas R. "The Brothers Niebuhr: Some Life-Long Differences." *Princeton Seminary Bulletin* (Summer 1974) 34–35.

McGuire, John M. "Few in Wright City Remember Niebuhr." *St. Louis Post-Dispatch* (June 18, 1992).

Messenger of Peace. "Sister Adele Retires." *Messenger of Peace* [monthly newsletter of Peace Memorial Evangelical and Reformed Church, Chicago] (Apr. 1941) 1–3.

Moltmann, Gunther. "The Pattern of German Emigration to the United States in the Nineteenth Century." In *America and the Germans: An Assessment of a 300-Year History,* edited by Frank Trommler and Joseph McVeigh, 1:14–24. Philadelphia: University of Pennsylvania Press, 1985.

Niebuhr, Christopher. "Letter to John Clifford Helt." Oct. 11, 1991. In the author's possession.

Niebuhr, H. Richard. "A Communication: The Only Way into the Kingdom of God." *Christian Century* 49 (Apr. 6, 1932) 447.

———. "The Grace of Doing Nothing." *Christian Century* 49 (Mar. 23, 1932) 378–80.

———. "In Memory of My Co-Worker 'Pat.'" Unpublished manuscript, photocopied, n.d. In the author's possession.

———. *The Kingdom of God in America.* New York: Willett, Clark and Co., 1937.

———. "Letter to Carol Niebuhr Buchanan." Apr. 25, 1959. Copy in the author's possession.

———. "Letter to Carol Niebuhr Buchanan." Feb. 11, 1961. Copy in the author's possession.

———. "Letter to Reinhold Niebuhr." N.d. In Reinhold Niebuhr Papers, Library of Congress, Washington, DC.

Bibliography

Niebuhr, H. Richard, et al. *The Church against the World.* Chicago: University of Chicago Press, 1935.

Niebuhr, Hulda. *Greatness Passing By: Stories to Tell Boys and Girls.* New York: Scribner's Sons, 1931.

———. "Letter to June Bingham." May 3, 1954. In Reinhold Niebuhr Papers, Library of Congress, Washington, DC.

———. "Letter to Theodore Braun." Jan. 31, 1959. In Reinhold Niebuhr Papers, Library of Congress, Washington, DC.

———. "Letter to Theodore Braun." Feb. 3, 1959. In Reinhold Niebuhr Papers, Library of Congress, Washington, DC.

———. *Ventures in Dramatics: With Boys and Girls of the Church School.* New York: Scribner's Sons, 1935.

Niebuhr, L. "Week-Day Activities." In *Sunday School Work in the Evangelical Synod of North America, 1916-1919: Official Report of the Second National Convention of Evangelical Sunday Schools*, by Board of Sunday Schools, 131-32. St. Louis: Board of Sunday Schools, 1919.

Niebuhr, Lydia. "Letter to Carol Niebuhr Buchanan." Jan. 2, 1961. Copy in the author's possession.

———. "Letter to D. B. Robertson." Jan. 20, 1959. In D. B. Robertson Papers, Syracuse University archives, Syracuse, NY.

———. "Letter to John Finlayson." Feb. 1, 1954. In the author's possession.

———. "Postcard to Eleanore Merckel." Sept. 8, 1930. In the author's possession.

———. "The Training School for Service." In *Report of the Second National Convention of the Evangelical Women's Union* [Elmhurst College, Elmhurst, IL, July 24-26, 1923], 89-93. Unpublished manuscript, typed. In Eden Theological Seminary archives, Saint Louis.

Niebuhr, Reinhold. *Beyond Tragedy.* New York: Scribner's Sons, 1937.

———. *The Children of Light and the Children of Darkness.* New York: Scribner's Sons, 1944.

———. *Christ and Culture.* New York: Harper and Brothers, 1951.

———. *Christianity and Power Politics.* New York: Scribner's Sons, 1940.

———. *Does Civilization Need Religion?* New York: Macmillan Company, 1927.

———. "The Failure of German-Americanism." *Atlantic* (July 1916) 16-18.

———. "Faith for a Lenten Age." *TIME* (Mar. 8, 1948) 70-79.

———. *An Interpretation of Christian Ethics.* New York: Scribner's Sons, 1935.

———. *Leaves from the Notebook of a Tamed Cynic.* New York: Willett, Clark and Company, 1929.

———. "Letter of Resignation." In Bethel church bulletin, Apr. 22, 1928. In Immanuel-Bethel United Church of Christ archives, Royal Oak, MI.

———. "Letter to Beulah Niebuhr." Sept. 26, 1946. In Carol Niebuhr Buchanan's possession.

———. "Letter to Beulah Niebuhr." Feb. 14, 1961. Copy in the author's possession.

Bibliography

———. "Letter to June Bingham." Feb. 7, 1961. In Reinhold Niebuhr Papers, Library of Congress, Washington, DC.
———. *The Meaning of Revelation*. New York: Macmillan, 1941.
———. *Moral Man and Immoral Society*. New York: Scribner's Sons, 1932.
———. "Must We Do Nothing?" *Christian Century* 49 (Mar. 30, 1932) 415–17.
———. *The Nature and Destiny of Man*. 2 vols. Gifford Lectures, 1939. New York: Scribner's Sons, 1941, 1943.
———. *Reflections on the End of an Era*. New York: Scribner's Sons, 1934.
———. *The Reminiscences of Reinhold Niebuhr*. New York: Columbia University Oral History Research Office, 1972.
———. *Young Reinhold Niebuhr: His Early Writings, 1911–1931*. Edited by William G. Chrystal. St. Louis: Eden, 1977.
Niebuhr, R. Gustav. "Letter to John Clifford Helt." Mar. 29, 1993. In the author's possession.
Niebuhr, Ursula M. "Letter to John Clifford Helt." Apr. 13, 1988. In the author's possession.
———. *Remembering Reinhold Niebuhr: Letters of Reinhold and Ursula M. Niebuhr*. New York: HarperCollins, 1991.
Nollau, J. "Clara Elisabeth Hosto (née Kamphoeffner)." [In German.] *Friedensbote* 52 (Oct. 13, 1901) 324.
Rasche, Ruth Weltge. "Uncle Albert Hosto in California." Unpublished manuscript, single typed page, n.d. In the author's possession.
Redeker, Martin. *Schleiermacher: Life and Thought*. Philadelphia: Fortress, 1973.
Schmidt, Henry J. "The Rhetoric of Survival: The Germanist in America from 1900–1925." In *America and the Germans: An Assessment of a 300-Year History*, edited by Frank Trommler and Joseph McVeigh, 2:204–16. Philadelphia: University of Pennsylvania Press, 1985.
Schneider, Carl E. *The German Church on the American Frontier*. St. Louis: Eden, 1939.
———. *History of the Theological Seminary of the Evangelical Church*. St. Louis: Eden, 1925.
Schulz, Florence. "Letter to John Clifford Helt." Oct. 1986. In the author's possession.
———. "Letter to John Clifford Helt." Apr. 6, 1988. In the author's possession.
Scott, Anne Firor Scott. *Making the Invisible Woman Visible*. Urbana: University of Illinois Press, 1984.
Smith, Ella Mae. "Interview with Elizabeth Caldwell." Audiotape, 1988. In the author's possession.
Stanger, Robert. "1871–1971: The First One Hundred Years." Special issue, *Elmhurst College Magazine* (Jan. 1971).
Stein, K. James. *Philipp Jakob Spener: Pietist Patriarch*. Chicago: Covenant, 1986.
St. John's Evangelical Church. "The Service of Thanksgiving in Commemoration of the Fiftieth Anniversary of the Deaconess Hospital, Lincoln, Illinois."

Bibliography

Printed program, June 22, 1952. In St. John United Church of Christ archives, Lincoln, IL.

———. *St. John's Evangelical Church: Souvenir of the Seventy-Fifth Anniversary Celebration.* Pamphlet, Oct. 15, 1933.

Stone, Ronald H. *Professor Reinhold Niebuhr: A Mentor to the Twentieth Century.* Louisville: Westminster John Knox, 1992.

Stringer, Lawrence B. *History of Logan County.* 2 vols. Chicago: Pioneer, 1911.

Sweet, Leonard I. *The Minister's Wife: Her Role in Nineteenth-Century Evangelicalism.* Philadelphia: Temple University Press, 1983.

W. "Mrs. Elizabeth Anna Weltge." *Messenger* (Oct. 15, 1936) 14.

Weston, William J. "Ironic Protestantism at *Home*: Christian Realism and Family Life." Paper presented to Southern Sociological Society, Centre College, Danville, KY, Apr. 18, 1992. In the author's possession.

Wolf, Stephanie Grauman. "Hyphenated America: The Creation of an Eighteenth-Century German-American Culture." In *America and the Germans: An Assessment of a 300-Year History*, edited by Frank Trommler and Joseph McVeigh, 1:62–76. Philadelphia: University of Pennsylvania Press, 1985.

www.ingramcontent.com/pod-product-compliance
Lightning Source LLC
Chambersburg PA
CBHW071623170426
43195CB00038B/2087

"John Helt brings the life and ministry of Lydia Hosto Niebuhr out of the shadows. This biography of her great influence both in her family and in the church is told with vivid examples. Anyone who is interested in the theological contributions of her sons and daughter should read this book and see how the seeds were planted within her family and nurtured with her tender and fierce care."

—**Elizabeth Caldwell**, author of *A Mysterious Mantle: The Biography of Hulda Niebuhr*

"This beautifully written and timely book brings to light the life of a 'reverent spirit' and servant of the gospel who helped shape the faith of several generations as one in whom, as Saint Jerome once put it, 'the lips, the heart, and the hands agree.'"

—**Frederick Trost**, author of *The Evangelical Catechism: A New Translation for the 21st Century*

"John Helt is himself a wise and discerning son of the German Evangelical Pietistic tradition of which he writes. Here he narrates the centrality of Lydia Niebuhr, mother of Reinhold and Richard, as a key force in the nurture of that Evangelical tradition in the United States. Helt invites appreciation and gratitude for this strong woman of faith who bore lifelong energetic witness to the life-giving force of the gospel."

—**Walter Brueggemann**, professor emeritus of Old Testament, Columbia Theological Seminary